Readymade Interview Questions

Readymade Interview Questions

MALCOLM PEEL

KOGAN
PAGE

First published in Great Britain in 1988 by
Kogan Page Limited, 120 Pentonville Road,
London N1 9JN

Reprinted 1989

British Library Cataloguing in Publication Data

Peel, Malcolm
    Readymade interview questions.
    1. Personnel. Interviewing – Manuals
    I. Title
    658.3'1124

    ISBN 1-85091-709-4
    ISBN 1-85091-708-6 Pbk

Printed and bound in Great Britain by
Biddles Ltd, Guildford and King's Lynn

Contents

post to be filled 68; Is all well? 70; Building a smooth
bridge 72

Introduction

The selection situation

Selecting someone with whom we intend to become closely involved is one of the most difficult decisions we can make.

Such decisions crop up in many situations. In private life, we make them when choosing friends, marriage partners or club members; in business life, we make them when choosing staff, suppliers, partners, associates or agents.

The difficulties of selection

Most of us grow up with the feeling that 'we know how to pick the good ones'. But if we are wise, time and experience bring humility. We learn a little about the complexity of human character and relationships. We learn something of the problems of trying to predict behaviour, especially in a new environment, and we find out that there can be no short cuts, and at the end of the day no certainty in choosing people. Unfortunately, irreparable damage may have been done before these realisations dawn.

Picking a wrong 'un is bad enough, but its consequences pale into insignificance compared with the results of failing to spot a winner.

The cost of selection

Choosing someone for a post is a major capital investment. The costs include:

- advertising
- agency or consultant fees (if used)

- management and administrative time, including
  - documentation
  - short-listing
  - interviewing
  - induction
- candidates' expenses
- relocation (if paid)
- loss of effective work during the learning period (the 'learning curve').

For a senior post, these are likely to total many thousands of pounds.

The opportunity cost of failing to pick the best person can be even higher. Not only will we lose the pay-off from their skills, but one of our competitors will be sure to gain it. In a top level job, the cost of losing opportunities for expansion and growth that our competitors gain may be almost infinite. If we make this error, the entire future of our organisation may be destroyed at a stroke.

The problems of rectification

'Appoint in haste, repent at leisure' is a motto worth a place on the wall of every selector. Putting things right after a mistaken selection may be traumatic.

Discovering the failure will involve assessing performance accurately and quickly. Facing the discovery will call for moral courage and interpersonal skill. Getting rid of the person will present procedural difficulties and possibly legal aspects. Even at its easiest, the termination process will be highly unpleasant.

There will also be direct costs. We will lose from the mistakes and poor performance during the period of employment. There may be physical damage, waste, lost business, upset customers or demotivated colleagues. Compensation might be payable, and perhaps wages in lieu of notice. At the end of it all, we will have to face a second round of expense in trying to make a better choice.

The two-way fit

Selection involves matching people and jobs. But there are two sides to every match: the satisfaction of the employer and the satisfaction of the candidate. Both must decide how close the match appears. Both must try to foresee the future. Both are entitled to their opinion. Either or both may make a mistake, and whichever it is, the damage will be equally serious.

Employers have traditionally tended to be arrogant. They have felt, if only subconsciously, that they were conferring a favour on the candidate they were pleased to choose. If the market conditions allow, they may pressurise candidates into accepting unfair offers. They may make false claims about what the job offers, or fail to point out its drawbacks or difficulties.

Candidates may make unjustified claims about the level or extent of their experience. They may go beyond the bounds of honesty, claiming false qualifications or hiding material facts. They may play employers off against one other.

When any of these things happen, the risk is the same, and both parties stand to suffer. Selection cannot be one way; the employer is choosing an employee, and the candidate is choosing an employer. Both are making a serious and difficult decision. Both will need to use all their skill and every aid available to have the best chance of success.

The plan of this book

The principal aim of this book is to supply a fund of tried and tested interview questions. But to use these questions effectively, we must put them into context. Good questions are of no value by themselves; used wrongly, they may even do harm. They must be asked correctly and sensitively at the right time, as part of a systematic and thorough process.

The book is therefore planned rather like Chinese boxes. It approaches the questions by stages. Part 1 looks at the interview process, and Part 2 suggests readymade questions, stage by stage.

1. The selection process
The outer box is the whole selection process; this is summarised briefly in Chapter 1. Those readers who are already familiar with the process will wish to pass over this ground quickly. Those who wish to know more are recommended to read the many excellent books listed in the Bibliography.

2. Selection interviewing

The next box is the process of selection interviewing which is, of course, only one part of the selection process. It is described in some detail in Chapter 2. Those who are familiar with the situation may wish at least to glance through what is said to see how closely their own ideas match the approach suggested there. Those who wish to study the subject in greater depth may wish to select additional reading from the Bibliography.

3. Questioning

The next box, Chapter 3, contains a description of the art of using questions in selection interviewing. To get the best value from the questions offered in Part 2, readers are recommended to devote time to this chapter.

The questions

Part 2, Chapters 4 to 10, contains suggested questions that the reader can choose and adapt for his own interviewing purposes.

As asking questions is of no value by itself, each question is followed by a selection of typical answers, to each of which a possible interpretation is given.

It is not suggested that all the questions are used for each candidate; this would be ineffective and impracticable. The hope is that readers will select from the questions offered those that meet their needs best. Some will be selected in advance, as part of the preparation for each interview. Some may suggest themselves, as the interview proceeds, to the reader who has become familiar with the book and its approach.

The reader will not find trick questions, designed simply to catch the candidate out, or load him with embarrassment. Such questions rarely help, and may well hinder good selection.

Sexism

Throughout the book, I have used 'he', 'his', 'him' etc. This is *not* intended to be sexist, but to avoid continual and tiresome repetition of he or she and the rest, or tying the reader and myself into knots with complex circumlocutions.

Acknowledgement

I would like to offer my most sincere thanks to Nick Parker of the Management Information Centre of the British Institute of Management for his invaluable help in preparing the Bibliography.

PART 1
THE PROCESS

1
THE RECRUITMENT PROCESS

To be successful, the recruitment process must follow a number of steps. These are:

1. Defining the job
2. Establishing the person profile
3. Making the vacancy known
4. Receiving and documenting applications
5. Designing and using the application form
6. Selecting
7. Notification and final checks
8. Induction.

Defining the job

Unless we know why we need to recruit someone, there can be little hope of succeeding. Everyone involved must know, and agree with everyone else, what job is to be done.

Is the job necessary at all?

The first question to be asked will always be 'Is there really a post to be filled?' When a vacancy occurs, we think automatically of filling it. But the post may not have been necessary, either because there was insufficient work, or because the work that was being done was unnecessary. The vacancy offers an ideal opportunity to examine the situation, and possibly to restructure what work is done and who does it in such a way that no recruitment is needed.

The job description

Most larger organisations have written job descriptions for each post.

Smaller organisations and individual employers may not have written descriptions. But even in the smallest organisation, the discipline of writing a description will help us to clarify our own thinking, and to communicate effectively with everyone else involved.

At the least, the description will need to cover:

- job title
- the purpose of the post
- who it reports to
- the duties and responsibilities.

Depending on our needs, we may also include:

- department
- grade or salary range
- for whom responsible
- relationships with other departments/posts
- external relationships.

The dangers of job descriptions

The existence of a vacancy gives us an opportunity to take out, dust down, read and update the job description. The manager responsible for the post, the professionals of the personnel department, and the outgoing occupant will all have something to contribute to this task. There are several shortcomings to look out for.

The description may not be up to date. The job will need to be structured and described for the next occupant, not as it was for the last.

The description may give little guidance as to what is actually to be done; how the job holder should fill his time. For effective recruitment, we may need to enlarge the description or supplement it with additional information.

The description may be too rigid and restricting. The way many posts work may legitimately depend on the skills and interests of the job holder. This may be the case, for example, with creative, academic or professional posts, or when an area of work is split between a number of similar positions. In such situations, good job descriptions need to be flexible, although we must not allow this to be an excuse for woolly thinking.

Now and then, the attempt to write a job description may cause a fundamental change in our thinking; perhaps the post could be abolished; maybe we need three separate posts; perhaps the whole area of work should be restructured; perhaps our requirements are impossible to meet.

The person profile

Having defined the job, we must picture the person who would best fill it. The result of this thinking is often called a person specification, but to many ears the word 'specification' sounds too scientific and inhuman; 'profile' may be better.

Generating possible factors

The best start for this part of the process is a clean sheet of paper and a sharp pencil, or if several people are involved, a flipchart pad and a marker. With these, we can jot down as many characteristics, skills, qualifications, aspects of experience, achievements, abilities, performance indicators, or whatever, that seem desirable in the person we are seeking. This phase should be done quickly and without criticism.

Revising the list

The next stage is to look back critically over what has been written in order to:

- cut out unsuitable factors
- add factors that have been overlooked
- eliminate duplication and overlapping
- clarify and tighten the wording.

Identifying pass/fail factors

Our choice will be made easier if candidates can be measured against pass/fail factors. If a candidate fails such a factor he will be eliminated from further consideration, thus making a first step towards our choice. This will be particularly useful if the factors can be judged on paper, without the trouble and expense of interviewing.

Of course, pass/fail factors must not be invented for the sake of it, or perfectly good candidates will be eliminated.

It is essential that pass/fail factors can be measured and predicted objectively. 'Must be of smart appearance', 'articulate', or 'credible to senior management', for example, cannot be used as pass/fail factors, however important they may be, because they are subjective and can be neither measured nor predicted.

The factors that we do not identify as pass/fail factors are 'desirable' factors. It is useful to weight these according to their importance in making the correct decision. A weight of 10 (or 20, or 100) can be given to the most important factor, and the remaining factors measured against it. There may, of course, be more than one factor with the same weight, and there may be gaps, sometimes large gaps, between the weights given to different factors.

We can conclude by rewriting our list, with the pass/fail factors first, and the desirable factors in order of their weights. This is our person profile.

Making the vacancy known

We will want the largest number of *suitable* candidates to be aware of and apply for the vacancy. But the fewer *unsuitable* candidates the better; they clog up the works and raise expectations that cannot be fulfilled.

The vacancy can be made known by:

- word of mouth
- internal advertisement
- external advertisement
- jobcentres or PER
- private agencies, consultants or headhunters.

Word of mouth
This method must not be neglected. Many vacancies are filled by candidates who have learnt of them from friends, colleagues or neighbours. Many a boss has dropped a hint (whether for positive or negative reasons) by drawing a vacancy to the attention of one of his people.

It may be objected that word of mouth is unfair, as some people may be denied the chance to apply for the vacancy. This is true; it may or may not matter. If fairness is essential, as may be the case in public appointments or when promotion is awarded on merit within an organisation, word of mouth must be supplemented by correct, adequate advertising. In such cases, justice must both be done and be seen to be done.

Internal advertisement

Many organisations fill vacancies from their existing staff whenever they can, and use a procedure to ensure that this policy is followed.

This usually involves the publication of single job advertisements or regular lists of vacancies. Such advertisements will not usually need to be as detailed as external advertisements, as the background and such matters as salary and conditions of employment will generally be well known to possible candidates.

External advertisement

Candidates are frequently sought through advertisements.

Factory gate notice-boards may be used to display a list of current vacancies, although this medium is usually restricted to unskilled jobs.

Less specialised jobs which are likely to be filled by those already living within easy travelling distance may be advertised in local newspapers. Higher level and more specialist posts may be advertised in national newspapers, and senior specialist posts may be advertised in the appropriate professional journals.

National advertising is a costly business, and an early and painful decision will be needed as to how much space can be afforded. It may also be difficult to obtain space in the better known national papers at short notice, although this problem may be overcome by using the services of a recruitment agency that regularly takes space.

Writing effective recruitment advertisements is harder than it seems. The descriptions of both the organisation and the post should be clear and attractive, but sufficiently tight to discourage unsuitable applications. Because advertising is expensive, they must also be brief. Display advertisements are the most costly, but are usually much more effective. For these, the format should catch the eye, but the style should be appropriate to the organisation and those it wishes to attract.

There may be commercial or political reasons for anonymity, and a decision about whether or not to reveal the name and address of the organisation in the advertisement will have to be taken.

The way in which the salary is described will need to be thought about. Some recruiters deliberately give no indication, and wait for the replies to show them what they will have to pay. However, this may waste time by attracting applicants with salary expectations that are too high or too low, and the best practice is probably to give an indicator: 'c£10,000' (c = circa 'about').

We must also make clear what information is needed from applicants, and in what form. Are we prepared to discuss matters on the telephone? Do we want potential applicants to ask us for additional details before applying? Should they send a CV (curriculum vitae) or do we prefer that they should request and use our application form? We may also indicate the deadline for the receipt of applications.

Ideally an advertisement should attract a small field of highly suitable candidates; between 20 and 30 is usually considered a good response. If there are many more, we have probably worded the advertisment too loosely, and handling the flood of applications will waste a lot of time.

Jobcentre or PER

Jobcentres can offer quick and efficient help with less specialised vacancies. The staff of the Centre will advise on the wording of the advertisement, which will be displayed in the Centre, and drawn to the attention of suitable job hunters. The service is free. It can be effective within the local area, but may be less helpful when the selection criteria are more demanding.

The PER (Professional and Executive Register) covers more skilled posts, and will advertise them in its regular, countrywide listing *Executive Post*.

Both these methods can be used to back up other methods of advertising.

Private agencies, selection consultants or headhunters

The word 'headhunter' is often used loosely. In fact, there are three distinct methods of operation, properly described by different names.

The *agency* operates by building up a file of people who may be interested in and qualified for certain kinds of vacancy (eg typists, computer operators, accounts clerks etc). It will usually interview people before putting their details on its files.

The agency can then respond to requests by employers for staff by submitting details of those who match their needs, and if required, arranging for them to be considered for selection. An agency may also approach employers, offering to put them in touch with staff on their books who may be suitable for their needs.

An agency will be paid by the employers who engage staff introduced to them by the agency, usually on the basis of a percentage of salary. Should the employee leave within a specified time, payment would be wholly or partly refunded. By law, agencies must not charge applicants.

The *selection consultant* may build up a register in the same way as an agency, but works primarily by accepting a brief to help fill a specific vacancy for an employer. He will carry out the first stages of the selection process on behalf of the employer; preparing and placing advertisements, receiving applications, long-listing, carrying out preliminary interviews and producing a fully documented short list. The employer will complete the selection by conducting final interviews (at which the consultant may or may not be present) and making the choice.

The selection consultant also will be paid on the basis of a percentage of salary, together with any costs, such as advertising and candidates' travel expenses, that have been incurred.

Use of a selection consultant enables the employer who does not recruit regularly to save time and effort, and to make use of the skills of the consultant, particularly in specialised areas. It also allows the employer to preserve anonymity until the later stages in the process.

The *headhunter* proper operates by accepting a brief from an employer to help fill a specific vacancy, which is usually at a high level or requires unusual skills or experience. He will then try to find and interest suitable candidates, by direct personal approach or approaches through mutual contacts. The process is usually conducted in the strictest confidence and will not involve advertising.

Receiving and documenting applications

Each application is of the greatest importance to the applicant, and may be of the greatest importance to the employer. Handling applications thus requires care, accuracy, speed and courtesy.

If someone complains (as a rejected candidate may, either directly, or perhaps to the Equal Opportunities Commission) it will be essential that all documents are available and in good order. We must therefore have a system to ensure that everything is received, read, registered, replied to and dealt with swiftly and carefully.

The steps we will have to take include the following.

Registration and filing

It is a good idea to give each vacancy a unique reference number. We can then endorse every application, and all the papers relating to it, with the reference number and the date we received them. We can also keep a register in which we record receipt of each application and all the subsequent actions we have taken; acknowledgements and other correspondence, dates of first, second and other interviews, the decision, the date the candidate was told of the result, the reply received, the taking up of references, medical examination, and joining the organisation.

We will need to file all papers and keep them for several years.

Acknowledgement

We will want to acknowledge applications and other correspondence at once if, as is often the case, we are unable to give a full reply. This will lessen applicants' natural anxiety, and show our professionalism.

Interview notes and test results

Some organisations use a standard format for interview notes to be completed at each interview. Whether we use this or not, we should make good notes, register them, and keep them on the file.

If we use any tests or examinations (including medical examination), we will also need to register and file the results.

References
If we take up references these too will need to be registered and filed.

Designing and using the application form

The application form is very important in the selection process. We can use it in the early stages to decide whether to take applications further; for the basic posts, we may even use its completion by the candidate as a simple test of literacy. It will help us to prepare for and conduct the interview. If we employ the candidate, it will form a permanent record with the significance of a contract between him and us. If we were to find that any important facts (eg qualifications, periods of experience etc) had been seriously misstated, we might decide to terminate his employment or take other action.

Design
If we design our own application form, we will need to make sure that it calls for all the information we will need. We must have enough to:

- decide whether to call the applicant for interview
- help to structure the interview
- enable us to take up references and check qualifications
- form the basis for a contract of employment.

But the form should also be easy for the applicant to complete and easy for us to use. To combine these requirements takes much thought. The exact wording of questions can be important, as can the order in which the form asks them. It should also appear tidy and uncluttered, and give sufficient space for replies.

The information we need for specialist and senior applications will be more detailed than the information we need in filling unskilled posts, and it is usually best to have two or three different forms for different levels of recruitment.

Use
We may send an application form to all serious applicants before interview. But if sufficient details are given in the letter of

application or curriculum vitae, we may leave completion until a later stage; perhaps after the first interview.

Selecting

The process of selection is most commonly carried out by matching and comparing candidates against the person profile, using the information given by the paperwork and what we learn at one or more interviews. The best use of the interview is the main subject of this book.

However, other sources of information may be helpful. They include:

- examinations and written papers
- performance tests
- personality tests.

Examinations and written papers

These are most commonly used in two situations:

1. Where a basic standard (eg of literacy or numeracy) is required, and we do not feel that qualifications claimed are an adequate or up-to-date guide. This is most likely for jobs such as clerical positions.

2. We may use written papers as part of the selection process for higher level posts requiring creativity, literacy and the ability to conceptualise. We may ask for them before interview, and use them either as a basis for choosing whom we wish to interview or as a basis for discussion and questioning at interview.

Performance tests

Tests are available which can measure people's skill in performing various actions, such as driving a van or a fork-lift truck, using a typewriter or computer keyboard, writing shorthand etc. It is always worth reviewing the person profile to check whether such skills are part of the job requirements and if so seeking a test that can help.

Personality tests

Tests are available which are designed to explore personality traits. Some may only be used under licence by those who have been trained by the test provider.

The commonest of these tests establish general intelligence (IQ = intelligence quotient). Such tests have a long history, and can give a clear indication of the overall intellectual potential of candidates, which can be of great interest and may often be usefully compared with educational attainments and job history.

There is a wide range of other tests, each based on its own view of the human personality. Tests are available to measure dimensions such as introversion/extroversion, stability/instability, relaxation/tenseness and so on. Other tests take quite different approaches; one, for example (the Luscher Colour Test), is based on colour preferences. In every case, the development of the tests will include using them on sample groups to establish the range of responses that can be expected.

Some of these tests have a long and respectable history; others may have been devised for a particular situation, or possibly with insufficient development or defective thinking.

Whatever the pedigree of the test, it is unlikely to help us unless we know how test performance relates to performance in the posts we are filling, and we will often lack this knowledge. To demonstrate, for example, that a candidate is 'highly extrovert' does not help unless we also know how the degree of extroversion is related to how well others have actually performed in the job.

Notification and final checks

Recruitment is not complete when a choice has been made; we still have several important tasks to carry out. These include the following.

Negotiations

We must tell the chosen candidate, agree salary or other conditions and deal with any questions or doubts he may have. We will have to do this as quickly as possible, for good candidates move fast. Many a carefully made selection has come to nothing because the person chosen has accepted another offer before we got around to making ours.

In some selection situations (particularly if all the candidates have been interviewed by a panel on the same day) candidates may be asked to remain until a decision has been made, and the selected candidate has accepted the offer.

Telling the unsuccessful

After the offer has been made and accepted we will need to tell unsuccessful candidates the sad news. Sometimes it may be best to keep more than one candidate warm until matters have been finalised. There may be a later vacancy coming up, for which a rejected candidate appears suitable, or the one we have chosen may refuse the offer, if not immediately, then at some stage before negotiations are complete.

In all cases, we will need to treat rejected candidates caringly and courteously. This is not just simple humanity, but also enlightened self-interest. The way we deal with them will affect how they view us and our organisation; they may be customers or know customers; we may need them next time; one day they may turn up on the other side of the table.

Medical examination

It may be necessary for successful candidates to be medically examined. If so, this is best done immediately, before the candidate must give notice to his present employer.

References

References are useful in two ways; they can be used to cross-check what we have been told by the candidate and they can give us additional opinions about him.

They may be taken up (provided permission is given by the candidate) at any stage in the process, although it is usual not to take up references from the present employer until the very end, for obvious reasons.

Telephone references are now more commonly used, and many recruiters believe that they are more useful than written references, as comments may be made verbally that would not be committed to writing. However, some people will not give telephone references to those they do not know, and telephone conversations are not a permanent record.

Induction

The recruitment process ends when (and only when) the chosen candidate walks through the door on the appointed day, and is received happily into the mysteries of his new post. If this final stage goes wrong, all that has been done may be wasted.

2
THE INTERVIEW

We can think of a series of interviews as having five elements, several of which occur outside the interview room. They are:

1. Setting up the series
2. Individual preparation
2. The interview itself
4. Interpretation and decision-making
5. Documentation and note-taking.

Setting up the series

When the post is simple, or there are few candidates, a single round of interviews is often sufficient. If so, setting up the series is not likely to be difficult.

For more complex or senior posts, more than one round of interviews will be needed. The use of two stages allows the field of candidates to be reduced to a more manageable size, and performance at one interview to be compared with performance at another. Informal interviews may be added as a first stage, and for a senior post, or where a number of individuals or departments must be satisfied, it may be necessary to add a third round.

A common pattern is:

- informal interviews (if used)
- selection of the long list
- first interviews
- short-listing
- second interviews
- final selection.

When setting up the series, we must also think about:

- panel size and composition
- hardware and environment.

We may be able to carry out first and second interviews during one visit by the candidate, thus saving time and expense.

Informal interviews

We may decide that 'informal' interviews will help as an extra first stage. In this context, 'informal' means that all comers at an advertised place and time will receive an interview without appointment.

Informal interviews are useful when a number of similar posts are to be filled or when a shortage of suitable applicants is expected. Typically, they may help when an organisation moves to a new area, mounts a major expansion programme, or during graduate recruitment. They may be combined with a display or exhibition describing and promoting the organisation.

In the right situation, informal interviews can offer substantial advantages, attracting interest from potential candidates who would not otherwise apply, and making efficient use of selectors' time. Drawbacks may include overselling of the organisation or the jobs on offer, leading to waste of time at a later stage, or possibly mistaken decisions.

Selection of the long list

If the person profile includes pass/fail factors, these can be used to accept or reject applications as they are received. However, such 'preselection' can only be undertaken if the information given by candidates is adequate.

If there are no pass/fail factors, we will have to wait until the deadline has passed or the stream of applications has dried up before a long list can be produced. We will then decide by comparing applications against the desirable factors in the person profile, and inviting for interview those who seem the closest match.

We shall usually aim to go forward with a long list of between 10 and 20 candidates. If we have less, there is little to be gained from two stages, but to interview many more would be wasteful of money and time, unless similar posts are likely to become vacant in the near future.

First interviews

At the first interview our main objectives will be to eliminate unsuitable candidates and gather as much relevant information as we can about the others.

Many recruiters find that at this stage a one-to-one discussion makes the establishment of rapport between candidate and interviewer easier and speeds the flow of information.

Such an interview may be carried out by a personnel professional, who will concentrate on assessing general factors. If so, technical competence will be assessed at the second interview by specialist staff. On the other hand, when filling technical positions for which it is pointless to consider candidates who lack the required degree of competence, we may prefer the opposite approach. We may decide that it is more sensible for a specialist to assess technical competence at first interview, and follow this, for those candidates who do well, with a second interview to assess general suitability.

The planned length of first interviews will vary with the complexity of the post to be filled. The more complex or senior the post, the more information will need to be exchanged. In the case of senior posts, up to two hours may be necessary; longer than this, concentration will be difficult for both parties. Most people would regard 20 minutes as the minimum allowance for a first interview; the average length is between a half and one hour.

Keeping a series of interviews to time can be difficult. A buffer of between five and ten minutes per interview can be helpful to allow for overrunning.

Interviewing is a tiring activity that demands unwavering concentration, and the number of interviews planned for one day must depend on the stamina of the interviewer. From this perspective, the fewer interviews in a day, the better; six to eight is as many as most recruiters would tackle, and if the post is complex or senior, two or three may be the limit.

However, if a series of interviews extends over too long a period, memories of the earlier candidates become fogged and confused, and it is best to complete a series of interviews in three or four days at most.

The findings of the first interview will need to be written up for the benefit of later interviewers, giving the assessments made and the reason for those assessments.

Short-listing

Our aim will usually be to produce a short list of between four and six candidates.

Using the information obtained at first interview, and the general feel for the overall standard of the candidates, we will use the desirable factors of the person profile to help compare those we have seen. Additional factors may have surfaced during the interviews; if so, we must apply them equally to all the remaining candidates.

We will need to make the file notes about candidates whom we reject. These will be invaluable in case of query or complaint, if additional candidates are needed at a later stage, or if similar vacancies come up in the not too distant future.

Some recruiters prefer to inform those they decide are quite unsuitable as soon as possible, but we may decide not to tell the better candidates we plan to reject until we have made an appointment, in case we need them later.

Occasionally, we may feel that there are insufficient candidates of a satisfactory standard, and decide to advertise again before spending time on a further stage of interviews.

Second interviews

Second interviews are usually conducted by a panel, thus giving more of those involved a chance to meet the candidate, and to compare reactions to him.

All panel members must be clear who is in the chair, and what role they are each expected to play. They will need full sets of documentation. They must know what has been covered in the previous stages; in particular, they must be clear how far technical competence or specialist knowledge has been explored.

Second interviews do not usually need to be as long as first interviews, as the latter are expected to have covered the ground in depth. Forty-five minutes, including the buffer between interviews, is a common allowance. Less than half an hour is not usually felt to be enough, while more than an hour strains the concentration of both panel and candidate.

Final selection

It is usual to complete selection (subject to references and medical examination) on the same day as final interviews, while the panel is together and candidates are fresh in the mind.

Full documentation should be completed on all candidates, whether they are accepted or rejected.

Panel size and composition

One-to-one interviewing is common at the first stage of a multi-stage selection process. Rapport can be established more easily between interviewer and interviewee, and a natural flow of dialogue encouraged.

However, the relationship may be slanted or incomplete, because of lack of technical expertise on the part of the interviewer, or spontaneous liking or dislike between candidate and interviewer. Less experienced interviewers may also find it difficult to take sufficient notes as the interview proceeds.

Small panels of two or three are common. Frequently they will include a specialist in the relevant work and one or two generalists; perhaps a general manager and a member of the personnel function.

Such panels have many advantages. Each member will relate to the candidate in a different way. Members can, if they wish, adopt deliberately different approaches to the candidate (eg 'hard' and 'soft'). It is less likely that points will be overlooked. While one member is involved in dialogue with the candidate, the others can observe, listen and take notes. Afterwards, each interviewer will be able to check and compare his view of the candidate against those of the others.

Occasionally, a small panel may experience difficulty in developing rapport. Members of the panel may sometimes get in each other's way, either duplicating lines of questioning or missing areas out on the assumption others will cover them. They may fail to understand each other's methods, interrupting, interpreting or even answering a colleague's questions. Tensions may exist between panel members, and an over-dominant member may distort the result.

Large panels with six and more members have traditionally been used in some public services – local government, education and related areas. They enable many people to be involved in the selection, something which may be desirable in an organisation with elected members, possibly of several political parties, and permanent officials. The same may apply where a central office or an elected board is involved, or where the membership of a body (perhaps a club, political party or trade union branch) claims the right to participate in a selection.

The disadvantages of large panels arise from their clumsiness. It will be difficult for panel members to establish rapport with the candidate, or to pursue a consistent line of questioning. Political factors (with a large or small 'p') may make control difficult, and not all members may get a fair chance to ask questions. Panel members may go in for speechifying and the making of points in front of their colleagues. The procedure is loaded against candidates who do not enjoy public performance, even though this skill may not figure on the person profile.

Group interviews or discussions are sometimes used, in which a number of candidates will be watched by a panel of observers. The technique is most useful in exploring the social and interpersonal skills of candidates, and may also be used to test leadership skills.

The need to have all candidates present at the same time and to keep them until other elements of the process (such as individual interviews) have been completed may cause difficulties. For this reason, the technique is most commonly used when a number of similar posts are being filled at the same time, as with graduate intakes or in assessment centres.

Peer group interviewing, in which the panel is made up of potential colleagues or subordinates of the post being filled, is a less usual but interesting variant. It will usually be combined with more conventional interviews.

If peer group interviewing is not used, there should at least be an opportunity for candidates to tour the work environment and meet those who would be their colleagues.

Hardware and environment

The physical environment of an interview will affect its degree of success. The most skilful interviewing techniques will achieve little if deployed in an atmosphere of distractions and interruptions.

The aspects of hardware that matter most are:

- the reception arrangements
- the interview room
- furniture.

Reception arrangements are improved if security and reception staff have been alerted to the candidates' expected arrival.

We will need a decent waiting room, or at least a comfortable chair in our secretary's office. A choice of reading matter is welcome and can be useful; brochures or information about the organisation and its work will help to supplement any back numbers of *Punch* and *The Lady* we have been able to scrounge from our dentist's receptionist.

The candidate can be asked to fill in his expense claim or, if he has not already done so, an application form while he is waiting.

If one was not supplied with the application, we can also arrange for someone to take a photograph of the candidate at this point, preferably with a Polaroid camera. While this may occasionally embarrass a nervous candidate, it will be of great value to the panel.

The interview room must be private, free from interruption and distraction, and reasonably tidy and comfortable. We may have to use our office if it is the only place available, but few organisations are without better accommodation; committee, meeting or board rooms, or even special interview rooms.

The furniture and the way it is arranged can do a lot to establish the atmosphere.

Conducting an interview from behind a desk, especially your own, conveys a feeling of status, and the physical barrier will create a psychological barrier which makes rapport harder to establish.

A table may have the same effect, if the interviewer or panel sits on one side and the candidate on the other, especially if the candidate's seat is placed at some distance from the table.

If the interview is one-to-one, a good layout is two low chairs, arranged at 45 degrees to each other to avoid the feeling of confrontation.

Panel interviews can be conducted round a suitably sized table, but with seating arranged to avoid a feeling of opposition. A round table is ideal.

Problems with paperwork in such layouts can be minimised by using a clipboard.

Individual preparation

Lack of preparation is one of the biggest barriers to effective interviewing. However experienced we may be, it is impossible for us to interview effectively unless we have learnt all we can about each candidate and planned our strategy before we meet him.

Experienced interviewers usually familiarise themselves with the candidates' applications in three stages. The first stage will take place as early as possible, to allow time for necessary research and thought. The second stage will be undertaken 24 hours or so before the interview, and the final stage will be a quick refresher immediately before meeting the candidate.

In the *first stage*, the interviewer will consider each application individually in relation to the person profile. He may highlight information that seems significant or needs probing in the application form, CV or letter of application. He may list questions, or areas of interest that need exploration. He may conduct research of his own, either to check statements made (if he is able) or to ensure he has sufficient background.

He will develop a strategic plan for the interview, considering not only which areas he wants to explore, but how he can best do so. Strategy is particularly important if a panel is involved, and the interview will run more smoothly if the panel is able to meet together in advance.

In the *second stage*, the interviewer will revise his knowledge, note down the results of any research or thought, and think of the series as a whole rather than only of each individual candidate.

The *third stage*, immediately before meeting the candidate, ensures that the interviewer has fresh in his mind the candidate's name, present situation, place of residence, and any point about his CV which suggests common background.

The interview itself

The three levels
The interview is in some ways a charade played out by both parties on at least three levels.

At the *first level*, both are likely to pay lip service to the two-way nature of what they are doing. The employer will claim that he is anxious to give all the information to the applicant that the latter wants, that he is being scrupulously fair, that he will give every opportunity to the applicant to make his case in the best possible way, and so on.

The applicant will make out that he is being honest, truthful and open in all he says, and that his only desire is to prove to the employer's satisfaction that he really is the best choice for the post.

At the *second level*, both parties will know that the employer alone can offer or withhold the job.

The employer will regard everything said by the applicant with suspicion, unless and until he has established himself as credible.

The applicant will do all he can to bend the truth to his advantage, hiding his problems, and playing up his good points. He may even lie about material facts.

At the *third level*, if it is reached, both employer and applicant will realise that a mistake in what is being done would have serious, long-term consequences for both, that job selection is difficult, and that they would do well to help themselves by helping each other.

It is at this third level that both employers and candidates need to operate, but getting and staying there demands much understanding and will-power.

Style

The interview has been defined as 'a conversation with a purpose', but this begs an important question: are we engaging in a real dialogue when we interview, and aiming to set up a real relationship, or is the situation purely conventional, with strict limits and detachment on both sides?

If *genuine dialogue* is used, the aim is to use the interview as the potential start of a relationship which may subsequently grow. Because we are meeting someone who may work with us, our aim will be to lay the best foundations we can for a long-term, worthwhile relationship. The relationship may not, of course, develop, as either party may abort the process, but at this stage we do not know.

This approach is a sort of courtship. Both parties will put themselves forward in the best light, but without deception which might later jeopardise the relationship. Both will give of their personality, and seek to learn about the other. When subjects are discussed, real opinions will be exchanged, and warmth may develop. If difficulties are encountered, they will be talked through openly and constructively. Both parties will be prepared to change as the relationship grows. Both will develop a sense of obligation to the other for what has passed between them. Both will seek pleasure from the relationship.

To work, this approach to interviewing must be consistent both with the style of the organisation and the personality of the interviewer. The organisation must be open and informal, and the interviewer must be psychologically secure, mature and open in his approach.

It is easier to adopt this style in a one-to-one interview, and easier for a first than for a final interview. It may, however, be used by a panel, provided all members understand and accept it, and it is equally appropriate for any stage in the process.

The style is frequently used by selection consultants and headhunters, most of whom, while working for a client who pays them, feel the need to operate as an 'honest broker'.

In *conventional interviewing*, the interviewer deliberately establishes and maintains distance from the interviewee. No relationship is developed, and if any appears to be growing it is consciously suppressed. When subjects are discussed, the interviewer will take great care to withhold his own views. The interview is bound by conventions which set it apart from normal social situation; what happens in the interview room is separate from everything that happens outside.

This style of interviewing is appropriate for organisations with a rigid structure and a hierarchical management style. It is inevitable when individual interviewers lack the security and confidence to engage in real dialogue, and with larger panels or panels whose members are not free and open in their dealings with each other.

Conventional interviewing is not necessarily wrong or inappropriate. If the management style of the organisation is not open, open interviews would lead to wrong selections. Moreover, the conventional approach has the important advantage that selection is less likely to be based on personal bias, or that time will be wasted on irrelevant chatter or expressions of opinion by the interviewer.

Stress interviewing. The term 'stress interview' is occasionally heard. It has no precise meaning, but is used loosely to describe an interview in which the interviewee is put under deliberate pressure by the type of questions asked or their manner of asking.

Questions may be specifically aimed at areas of apparent problems, weaknesses or embarrassment, or they may be deliberately phrased to offend or convey insulting innuendoes.

Occasionally, sadistic or unskilled interviewers will adopt such an approach, justifying it, if at all, with the belief that they learn 'what a man is made of' by how he reacts. Most people feel, however, that for every piece of relevant information thrown up during such an interview there will be many more that are lost because of the defensiveness, hostility and lack of rapport that it produces.

The person profile may occasionally include factors which justify this approach; an ability to put up with personal insults from strangers being the most obvious. Luckily, such requirements are rare, and the need for 'stress interviewing' similarly unusual.

Keep control. Whatever style is adopted, the interviewer must retain control of the interview.

Interviews should achieve the objectives both of interviewer and interviewee. But it must rest with one party to establish and maintain control of the proceedings; if both try, the interview will rapidly degenerate into a trial of strength. The interviewer should naturally perform this role, as he is the host and has the initiative, at the end of the day, to make or withhold a job offer.

Who does the talking? In any interview, the interviewee should do most of the talking. No exact proportion is right or wrong, but a guide figure of 85 per cent interviewee and 15 per cent interviewer is usually not far out. There will be some phases, such as the introduction, in which the interviewer will have more to say.

The phases of the interview
There are three basic phases:

- the introduction
- methodical questioning
- the conclusion.

Each of these is described in more detail in the chapters that follow.

The introduction will include the welcome of the candidate, personal introductions, and clarification as to how much he knows about the organisation and the post to be filled. The interviewer will try to relax the candidate, establish rapport, and set up a natural conversational flow. It is *not* an objective of this phase to assess the candidate by the way he walks across the room, for example, or the way he shakes hands. Any temptation to do so should be firmly resisted.

Methodical questioning will usually constitute the bulk of the interview. Based on a clear plan (the use of the CV is suggested in the following chapters) it will aim to explore the interviewee's past, present and future and their relevance to the post to be filled.

The conclusion will offer the candidate a chance to clear up doubts and make any final points. It will be made clear what the remaining stages of the process are, roughly how long they will take, and end with a polite but non-committal farewell.

Interpretation and decision-making

A panel will always feel the need to comment on each candidate as soon as he has left the room. But usually it will be wise to hold back until all the candidates have been seen. The previous candidate may have seemed the perfect answer (or utterly dreadful, as the case may be) but just wait until you've seen the next one ...!

When the time comes, systematic interpretation will need not only a good memory, but good notes; especially if the series has been long, or the interviews spread over several days. If photographs of the candidates are available, their value will become manifest now.

The first try

Panels will usually try to achieve consensus, if this is possible. However, a quick ballot *before* can be useful to establish how near the panel is to agreement. If this approach is used, each panel member should be asked to rank the candidates in writing, to ensure he is not influenced, at this stage, by his colleagues' views.

With luck, the choice may be quite clear. If so, it will only remain to review the evidence, and ensure that nothing has been overlooked.

Traps to avoid

Usually, the choice is much less clear, and the decision will need thought and debate. If so, there will be several traps to avoid:

Recency. The panel may have forgotten earlier candidates, and over-value the claims of those they have seen more recently, particularly if the series has been long.

Skilled presentation. Candidates who have presented them-selves outstandingly well will be prominent in the panel's thinking, at the expense of the less articulate. If self-presentation figures on the person profile, this is valid, but if not it should not be allowed to influence the decision.

Domination. The panel may be dominated by one or two of its members, who may try to steamroller the others into a decision with which they do not really agree. This is specially likely if it is the most senior member who holds strong views.

Lack of process. Many panels have no systematic approach to making a collective decision, and the discussion can rapidly become unfocused, irrational and repetitive. If the decision presents difficulty, a clear and understood process is essential, and it is worth spending time agreeing this before starting to discuss the candidates. A decision-making process which many panels have found useful is:

A decision-making process

There are three stages:

1. A last check should be made, in the light of all the information now available, that candidates pass the pass/fail factors. Any who do not must be finally eliminated.

2. A comparison should be made of all remaining candidates against each desirable factor working by each factor in turn, not by candidates. Candidates should be ranked in the order in which they meet each factor. This process will be clearer if it is drawn up in the form of a matrix, with each column devoted to a candidate, and each row to a factor of the person profile. The rankings are then totalled for each candidate. The one with the highest total will be the one who appears to meet the criteria best, and will be the provisional choice.

3. The evidence for the provisional choice should now be reviewed, asking the questions:

'Does this choice seem sensible in the light of each aspect of the evidence?' and

'If we appointed this candidate, what can we foresee that might go wrong?'

Each stage of the discussion will be easier and more fruitful if a flipchart is used to make the process visible and to note contributions and conclusions. This will focus attention, restrain verbosity, clarify thinking and preclude back-tracking.

Some selection procedures involve telling candidates the result before they leave. While this has advantages, it may put pressure on the panel and produce a hurried and unsatisfactory result.

Documentation and note-taking

It is not possible to retain everything of significance that is said during even the shortest of selection interviews. The human brain is far less able to retain everything that passes during long, in-depth interviews for senior posts.

Even those gifted with the most exceptional powers of memory would be unable to select those passages during an interview which only subsequent events might render significant; statements, for example, which later replies indicated needed probing, or with which the claims of later candidates might need comparison. In a long series of interviews, we may well confuse and forget the candidates themselves, let alone the details of their interviews.

Effective interviewing therefore calls for every aid to memory we can sensibly enlist. The value of photographs has been mentioned. Audio or video recording has occasionally been considered, although virtually all interviewers reject it on the grounds that it would make interviewees (not to mention most interviewers) tense and artificial, and that the time required to analyse replays would be at least as long as the interview itself.

At the end of the day, the interviewer will be thrown back on the need to make comprehensive notes. This is not easy, and needs practice and the right approach.

Permission

Some interviewers, particularly at one-to-one interviews, feel happier if they have asked the interviewee's permission to take notes, or at least drawn his attention to the fact that they intend to do this. But interviewees expect notes to be taken, and if they have feelings on the subject will almost certainly see it as fair and professional.

Some candidates may take their own notes during the interview, something which conveys an air of considerable efficiency on their part.

The folding clipboard

A folding clipboard is ideal for holding the papers and notepad. We can shut it when not in use to ensure confidentiality. When using it, we can angle it to prevent the candidate reading it. We can raise it nearer to eye level, to minimise loss of eye contact while listening and writing.

Volume of notes

It is difficult to predict which event or reply during an interview may later prove to be important, so it is best to take quite full notes. However, we must not allow this to hinder the establishment of rapport and the flow of information.

An average 30–45 minute interview will usually produce at least one A4 sheet of notes.

Use quotes

There is a danger that, in summarising replies, we may also introduce unconscious bias. The nearer our notes can be to what is actually said, the better. We should try to write down replies which seem important in the exact words used.

Timing

The moment we choose to make a note can affect the interview.

If we are finding it difficult to get the flow going, it is best to postpone note-taking until things are easier.

The candidate will always spot the point at which we write a note, and will naturally try to guess what has been written and why. When he is giving us straightforward information, this will not matter, but if we are noting favourable or unfavourable replies, we should avoid drawing his attention to our action. It is a good idea to delay making this kind of note for a few moments until he is talking about something else.

Writing up

At the end of each interview, we shall need, before seeing the next candidate, to note any points we did not get down during the discussion, while they are fresh in our memory. If the organisation uses a standard post-interview form, this is the time to use it.

The process and results of the final decision-making session will also need recording on the papers.

3
ASKING QUESTIONS

Questioning is the essence of the interview. Information is what we are after, but questioning has other functions as well.

At interview, the question is the verbal signal through which the interviewer can:

1. Direct and control the course of the proceedings
2. Stimulate the thinking and memory of the interviewee
3. Obtain the information that he needs to make the selection.

Asking effective questions is not easy. How and when a question is asked are as important as the thought behind it. Moreover, we have not finished with a question when we have asked it. We must listen carefully to the reply, and record and interpret it. Depending on the results of this process, which must be completed on the run, our following questions may be modified. Questioning is an interactive, dynamic process.

The physical and psychological atmosphere in which a question is asked will alter the way it is heard by the interviewee, and the response it produces. The simplest question, such as:

□ **Are you sure?**

Will not sound the same in the torture chamber as in the office of a positive and supportive interviewer.

The atmosphere will be the product of many ingredients, including the interview hardware, the style of the interview, the sequence of questions and the tone of voice and body language of the interviewer. Hardware and style have been discussed in Chapter 2. Sequence and body language are discussed below.

Using questions effectively is an art and, like other arts, we can improve our skill by thought, study and practice. We can think of it usefully under four headings:

1. The types of question
2. Linking questions together
3. Listening to the replies
4. Body language.

The types of question

Questions belong to one of several types, depending on the way they are asked. A practical classification for interviewing is:

- the open-ended question
- the closed question
- the yes/no question
- the multiple question
- the leading question.

The open-ended question

This is a question which indicates an area of interest, but allows a range of possible replies. It is particularly valuable when *exploring* and *searching*, but not appropriate when *collecting* or *examining*. It may or may not be suitable for the process of *probing*.

In exploring a candidate's motivation, for example, we may ask of an event in his CV (a bad examination result, perhaps):

□ **How did you feel about that?**

In exploring his social skills, we may ask:

□ **What approaches did you find worked best in this kind of situation?**

Considering his intelligence (or creativity), we may ask:

□ **What was your thinking in those circumstances?**

The degree of openness can vary widely. At one end of the scale, we might consider starting an interview by asking a question such as:

□ **Tell me about yourself.**

offering the broadest possible latitude. At the other end of the scale, we may simply ask a question of the form:

□ **Why did you do that?**

The more open the question, the more appropriate it is for the early, exploratory stage of the interview, or of a particular phase.

An open-ended question can rarely, except as an admission of a serious lapse of memory, be answered '*I don't know*'.

Open-ended questions often (but not always) begin with 'How' or 'Why'.

The closed question

Closed questions channel the reply towards a precisely defined area. They are the right type for *collecting* and *examining*. They may be suitable for *probing*, occasionally for *searching*, but never for *exploring*.

We may ask, for example:

□ **What salary did they give you when you were appointed to that post?**
□ **How long did you do that job?** or
□ **Who was your boss at that time?**

Closed questions frequently begin with 'Who', 'What', 'When', 'Where' or phrases like 'How much', 'How many', or 'How long'.

The yes/no question

Yes/no questions are closed questions that, as the name implies, call only for the answer 'Yes' or 'No'. They are ideal for *collecting*, and may be used for *examining* and *probing*, but are quite unsuitable for *exploring*.

We may need to ask, for example:

□ **Did they give you a car with that job?**
□ **Are you prepared to travel abroad?** or
□ **Is your boy still at school?**

In practice, many interviewees tend to enlarge on their yes/no answer, even though this was not strictly required by the form of the question.

The multiple question

A multiple question has two or more parts:

□ **Please tell me what you think your main achievements in the job were, why they were so good, and what skills relevant to the present job they indicate.**

Such questions usually confuse the interviewee, and are rarely effective. We should split them into their constituent parts and ask each separately.

The leading question

A leading question tries to guide the interviewee towards or away from a particular answer.

We may ask:

□ **You weren't prepared to put up with that, were you?**
□ **I expect you were pleased about that, weren't you?** or perhaps
□ **I don't suppose you liked that very much?**

Leading questions indicate the attitude of the interviewer and point out the hoped-for reply, and are likely to produce unreliable answers and false information. They have little value in any phase of interviewing, and should be avoided.

Leading questions frequently, but not always, end with an additional phrase such as 'did you?', 'were you?', 'could you?' etc. They may contain judgemental words: 'bad', 'good', 'successful' etc. They may use an apparently open question or statement which is turned into a leading question by the tone of voice:

□ **And that was the end of the matter?**

Linking questions together

The way individual questions work will also depend on the order in which they are used.

No order is always right. We must be flexible and ready to change our approach according to circumstances. But as a starting point, we may plan to move through a logical sequence such as:

- collection
- exploration
- search
- probe

- examination (if used)
- check (if needed).

Collection

This aims to clear the ground by filling any blanks in our knowledge which might exist because the CV supplied by the candidate omitted something, because a section of the application form had not been fully completed, or because a subject did not seem to have been covered at a previous interview.

Collecting questions will be of the closed or yes/no type.

If, for example, we are thinking about the applicant's first job, we might ask:

- ☐ **You give your starting salary, but not what you finished on. What was that?** or
- ☐ **Did you report direct to the purchasing manager, or was there a section head between you and him?**

Exploration

Exploration begins with the definition of the territory to be explored, and goes on to discover and describe everything we can find out about that territory.

In selection interviewing, exploration will often be our first approach, both to the candidate as a whole, and to individual areas. We may begin by a general exploration of the candidate's CV. Later, we will explore particular periods of his working life. What, for example, was he really doing, thinking and achieving during his time with Black's?

The questions used during exploration will usually be open-ended. However, it can be productive to use a mixture of open and closed, even open and yes/no questions.

For the applicant's first job, we might ask:

- ☐ **Can you summarise for me your main duties in this post?** or we might try the sequence:
- ☐ **Looking back, do you feel this job has really helped your subsequent career?** (Yes/no question to focus the thinking and invite commitment)
- ☐ **Why do you say that?** (Follow-up open question)

Search

Searching differs from exploration in that we know what we are looking for, and that it is there somewhere. Our chances of finding whatever it is will be better the more tightly we can define the field of search.

In a selection interview, we will search for things which we know exist, but which are not readily available to us, and possibly not to the interviewee. These may include, for example, his long-term ambitions, the reason why he chose a particular subject of study, or why he left his first job.

The type of question used will vary according to whether the interviewer believes the information he seeks is consciously available to the interviewee. If he believes the interviewee may be genuinely unsure, either through lack of insight or fault of memory, he may use open, followed by closed questions. If he believes the interviewee knows, the immediate question may be closed or yes/no.

Typical questions might be:

- **How easy was it to get your ideas accepted from such a junior position?** (Focusing the thinking with an open question)
- **Was your solution actually implemented?** (Yes/no, assuming the interviewee is likely to know, or has had his thinking jogged by the previous question)

Probe

This is one of the interviewer's most powerful weapons. It is applied when we are unsure whether what we have heard is correct or complete; 'the truth, the whole truth, and nothing but the truth'. The aim of the probe is, as its name implies, to dig deeper.

This does not necessarily imply deceit on the part of the interviewee. Interviewees often make mistakes from nerves, failings of memory, failure to express themselves well, or because they themselves are unsure of the true answer; good interviewing often brings new insight to the interviewee. We must also be sufficiently humble to realise that we may have failed to hear, understand or record a previous answer correctly. We must be careful that in probing we do as little as possible to destroy the rapport that has been built up, and approach our probe so that we do not appear arrogant or dogmatic.

The probe may be needed at any time. If we are satisfied that what we have been told gives us what we wanted, there will be nothing to probe. Likewise, we shall pass over unimportant matters, even though they seem doubtful. On important matters, however, the greater our doubts, the more time, skill and effort we shall spend probing.

More interviews go wrong from lack of probing than from too much. Inexperienced interviewers may be nervous of the probe, but it is a legitimate tool of selection interviewing, and should be used when needed without fear.

There is no set form for a probe; it may use any type of question. Typical probes, related to the previous examples, might be:

- [ ] **You mentioned your section leader earlier; how did he react when you approached your manager direct on this project?**
- [ ] **I was particularly interested in your use of regression analysis for this application. Trying hard to remember my elementary statistics, I'm not sure how I could do that. Can you enlighten me?**
- [ ] **What savings did all this actually produce?**
- [ ] **Does that mean that one of your colleagues lost his job?**

Examination

Examination differs from probing in that both the questioner and the responder believe that the questioner knows the correct answer. It is the classic schoolroom technique. It is also a powerful technique in interrogation; the suspect will fear its use, among other types of question, as it may prove a trap to catch lying or inaccuracy. 'How much,' the victim will ask himself, 'does he really know?'

If there are 'correct' answers to his questions, about which he is certain, the selection interviewer may also choose to use examination among his other techniques. However, this will not often be the case.

Check

A check aims to ensure that we have heard and understood the reply to a previous question correctly. It can follow any other type of question.

Its use may interrupt the flow, and occasionally harm rapport, so it should not be used more often than really necessary. However, it is even more harmful to mishear an important answer. If we feel it is necessary, we may offer a brief apology, but accuracy is so clearly in the interests of the candidate that few will object.

The most effective check is to restate what we thought we heard. But we must do this without any comment, even implied by our tone of voice, to avoid planting doubts in the interviewee's mind which might cause him to revise his reply.

In the previous example, we might ask:

- □ **I see. You are saying that your manager found it easier to work with you direct because your section leader lacked depth of experience in this particular area?** or
- □ **Thank you. Your point, if I have grasped it correctly, is that the savings were available, but never actually made, as management were anxious to avoid industrial relations problems with a particularly militant shop steward?**

An alternative method of checking is simply to ask the same question again, after a suitable lapse of time. The interviewee may point out that the question has been asked before, in which case we will smile blandly, apologise briefly and quietly await the second reply.

Repetition and rephrasing

At any stage, the interviewee may fail to grasp our question. This may result from a bad choice of words, disconnected ideas, or simple inaudibility. The interviewee may have failed to listen effectively, or lack the intelligence or experience to understand.

Our first need will be to realise what is happening. If there is a deafening silence, or the interviewee asks for a repetition, this may not be too difficult. More frequently, however, the interviewee will try to make the best of a bad job, fearing he will be thought stupid if he admits to being puzzled, and we will need to be sufficiently alert to pick up the situation quickly.

Having done this, we will have a number of strategies to choose from. We can:

- interrupt and repeat our question
- interrupt and rephrase our question
- interrupt and ask a different question

- listen to what is being said, and repeat or rephrase the question when it is finished
- listen to what is being said, deciding why the mistake was made, what that adds to our knowledge of the interviewee, and whether it suggests a new line of questioning.

Which we choose will depend on the importance of the original question, the apparent significance of the error, our interest in what is being said, and the time available. Most interviewers will listen at least for a short time, before deciding which action to take.

Listening to the replies

There is no point in asking effective questions if we do not listen to the replies.

There are a number of aids to effective listening. They include:

- active listening
- avoiding preconceptions
- hearing between the lines
- summary and restatement.

Active listening

Listening must both be and seem to be active.

To be active, it will help our concentration to watch the speaker, note the body language, and maintain good (but not absolutely continuous or frighteningly intense) eye contact.

To be seen as listening actively, we must adopt an alert posture and expression, and react with appropriate nods, facial expressions, occasional encouraging noises and brief statements: 'I see', 'Right', 'Go on', 'Really!'.

With some candidates, the need may be to staunch the flow. In this case, the listening activities will go into reverse; the interviewer will glance pointedly at his papers or his watch, withhold noises of encouragement, and await the inevitable pause for breath which will allow him to break in.

Avoiding preconceptions

It is difficult to avoid preconceptions, but we should at least be aware of our own, and the power they may wield.

Research suggests that many interviewers judge candidates

within the first two minutes of an interview, often by such irrelevancies as the way they walk across the room, the strength of their handshake, whether they sit before being asked, or similar aspects of behaviour. Having done this, they hear the remainder of the interview as it were through the filter of this judgement, picking out replies which support the belief they have formed, and ignoring, forgetting or mishearing those that go against it.

We all tend to interpret identical behaviour by different people according to the way we read their character.

Thus, if we believe the candidate to be clever, we will interpret a long hesitation before answering a question as proof that he is carefully evaluating the question and choosing the best possible reply. But if we believe him to be stupid, we will interpret the same hesitation as lack of understanding and a slow mental reaction.

A witty reply by a candidate we have taken a liking to will be seen as an indication of his friendly and outgoing disposition; we will see the same response by a candidate we distrust as uncalled-for cheek.

When interviewing a candidate with a first class honours degree from a highly reputable university we may fail to pick up evidence that his degree did not cover the exact areas of knowledge we need, or that his subsequent job performance suggests serious gaps in his practical competence.

If we learn that the candidate has been decorated for bravery, or performed meritorious service for the destitute and suicidal, this knowledge may blind us to his execrable working record.

Many suitable candidates have been rejected because indication of early failure has blinded interviewers to later and stronger indications of growth, improvement and success.

The point goes deeper than saying that we all tend to judge by slim and irrelevant evidence. This is true, but even worse, we are actually in danger of hearing replies wrongly, or failing to hear them correctly. Let interviewers beware!

Hearing between the lines
In the story of Silver Blaze, Sherlock Holmes solves a mystery by noting that a dog did not bark in the night (thus proving that the crime was committed by its owner). When attempting to interpret written references and testimonials, it is essential to

note not only the positive statements that are made about the candidate, but to spot the gaps – the things that might be expected, but are not there. In the same way, hearing what is not said, but might have been, may be as important as hearing what is said.

Failure to say something may arise from innocent causes. The fault may be ours; perhaps we asked an involved or multiple question which confused the candidate.

On the other hand, it may be a deliberate evasion of a problem area, perhaps in the form of an attempt to draw the discussion on to more favourable ground for the candidate:

□ **Was it your decision to leave Smith Ltd in 1978, or did they ask you to leave?**

I got more and more fed up with the way they were treating me at Smith's. My boss was a thoroughly self-centred man, who was forever creeping to the directors. I felt the time had come for me to look around and work out what I really wanted from life. I had never made use of my training as a typesetter, and it seemed to me that was the way forward for me. I started looking for ways I could use my skill and get job satisfaction. I knew I was a first-rate printer.

We still don't know the answer.

Gaps in what is said are frequently less obvious, and not necessarily a direct failure to answer a question:

□ **Tell me about your time with Brown Bros.**

I enjoyed it a lot. They were terrific people there; a real good crowd. Everyone used to muck in, and we'd spend time together after work. The bosses were the same – no class distinction there, no status symbols. I still keep up with most of them, even now …

And the work?

Summary and restatement

The act of retelling what has been said, either in the same words or, more usually, in summary, is a useful aid to effective listening. Not only does this provide a check when there is any doubt (see page 52), but it helps to discipline the interviewer who sets himself the task of showing he has heard and understood.

It is, of course, tedious and unnecessary to repeat or summarise every answer; we should only do so when doubt remains in an important area.

Body language

'Body language' has developed a mystique which may obscure its reality and make it appear a harder subject than it really is.

We all speak body language all the time; we cannot avoid doing so. Our body reflects our feelings. There is nothing special about this; we all know when someone is looking bored, tired or embarrassed. We all know how posture or small movements of the hands, fingers or lower limbs can show impatience or tension. We all spot and interpret the blush.

The effective interviewer will, however, pay particular attention to body language.

The body speaks louder than the voice
If the language of the rest of the body appears to contradict what the mouth is saying, we should not believe the mouth.

Language is the most sophisticated produce of the human intellect, and we spend much effort in refining and controlling our use of it. The rest of the body is a complex and comparatively primitive entity, over which we can only exercise partial control. If it indicates something different from our words, it is virtually certain to be nearer to the truth.

The interviewer must learn to look closely for signs of unexpected tension or other spontaneous reactions when interviewing. We will rarely see the candidate actually squirm when we probe a particular point, but we may well observe tension or anxiety in the hands or eyes, or by a shift of posture.

If the candidate expresses keen interest in some aspect of the job, or agrees with a statement we make, we will watch to see if his posture and expression tell the same story.

We must use our own body language effectively
To be fully effective as interviewers, we will need to ensure that our own body reinforces the message we wish to send, and does not contradict or overlay it with another message.

If we wish to appear interested and alert, for example, we must suppress the bodily signs of tiredness and boredom. If we wish to seem friendly and co-operative, we will suppress the spontaneous bodily reactions of disagreement, disbelief and agression.

In interviewing, our aim will be to encourage the interviewee to talk freely, especially during the early phases or if there appear to be difficulties. Body language will be of great help in this, just as it will help to silence an interviewee who is going on too long.

We will often wish to suppress our reactions to answers. If we show that we think a reply is good, we may spark off a stream of similar but insincere responses; if we show our dislike of something, the alert interviewee will rapidly adjust his future answers.

We can learn to observe and interpret the body language of others better

We all notice and interpret body language naturally. Some of us may be so sensitive to the language that it may be painful or embarrassing; we may find it difficult to continue a normal conversation with someone whose body language tells us they hate our guts. But some may be insensitive to such messages, and find themselves continually surprised when others react in a way they did not anticipate.

As with the spoken word, so we can all improve our sensitivity to body language by study, thought, and practice. We can do a lot simply by becoming conscious of the subject and making the most of our opportunities for observation and practice day by day. As interviewers we will take any opportunity to cross-check our reading by verbal questions, and in panel interviews we will discuss our observations with other panel members at the end of the interview.

If we wish to do more, there are a number of books and courses available.

PART 2
THE QUESTIONS

HOW TO USE THE QUESTIONS

The questions are readymade, but their use is up to the reader; used in the wrong way, at the wrong time, or of the wrong candidate, they may be useless or even harmful.

There are five headings in each of the chapters that follow:

- Overall objectives
- Sample questions
- Typical replies
- Possible interpretations
- Probes and supplementaries.

Overall objectives

These suggest the main aims of each phase of the interview. While we shall never exclude relevant information whenever we can get it, we must have a structure to what we are trying to do; the framework into which we will fit our questions.

Sample questions

It is obviously impossible to list questions that are suitable for all interviews. Some of those listed can be used as they stand in a wide range of situations, others will work well when adapted; yet others may suggest questions in the same general area that will help us.

To avoid repetition, questions throughout are set in **bold type**. Main questions are numbered; S indicates supplementaries.

Typical replies

It is even less possible to anticipate all the replies we shall receive. However, those offered are drawn from real life, and have been chosen as far as possible to illustrate typical attitudes and approaches that candidates are likely to take when faced with the question.

It will become clear, in most cases, which sort of response a candidate is making. However, we must be careful not to stereotype candidates, but to listen carefully to exactly what they say each time.

To avoid repeating the heading, typical replies are set in *italic type*.

Possible interpretations

The emphasis must be on the word 'possible'. The real meaning of any reply can only be found by fitting it in with all the other evidence we have; what the candidate has written, his other replies, his body language and presentation, references, reports, test or examination results. The interpretations suggested can, at best, do no more than help the reader to begin his own, unique approach to the unique individual he is with.

The heading is usually dispensed with, and the interpretation follows the *typical reply*.

Probes and supplementaries

In many cases, the possible interpretations are followed by suggestions for probes or supplementary questions.

In the more important areas, further typical replies and their possible interpretations are offered; in others, the continuation is left completely open.

A suggested method of working

To get the best value from this section, the reader may wish to follow a methodical process such as:

1. General preparation
Before starting any series of interviews, read at least Chapter 3; Chapters 1 and 2 if you are unfamiliar with the interviewing process. Then read the headings for Chapters 4 to 10, and those

complete chapters which you feel might be relevant to your needs. Read more than you feel you need rather than less.

2. Preparation for individual interviews
Before starting an individual interview, reread any chapters you feel might be particularly relevant in conjunction with the application and any other papers.

Draw up a simple outline plan of the way you would like the interview to go and the areas you wish to explore. Pick out questions, including supplementaries, that are related to those areas; copy them, adapting the wording carefully to the situation of the individual candidate, and decide approximately when you might use them. Read the likely replies and possible interpretations.

Remember, the replies are only samples of the infinite number you may get; make your own guesses as to what your candidate may say. Remember also that the interpretations are only suggestions. See how far you agree with them, and note where you disagree.

3. During the interview
Throughout the interview, listen carefully to the replies, and be ready to adapt your plan depending on what you hear. Do not use questions that have clearly become redundant or unsuitable. Using what you have learnt from the book and the approach it follows, add extra questions or supplementaries in what seems the best place.

4. Afterwards
Check your notes against the person profile, reinterpreting the replies to make a coherent picture of the candidate. Use the possible interpretations if they are helpful, but prefer your own if they are not.

5. Building experience
Annotate the book with your own comments and additional questions you may have used successfully, to help you next time.

However, never allow yourself to become rigid or to stereotype candidates; approach each one with an open and flexible mind, and improvise and adapt your questions, building on your own accumulating experience as well as the suggestions in this book.

4
THE OPENING

Overall objectives

1. Welcome and introductions.
2. Establishing rapport.
3. Ensuring that the candidate understands the selection process.
4. Checking what the candidate knows about the organisation, and giving any necessary information.
5. Checking what the candidate knows about the post to be filled, and giving any necessary information.
6. Ensuring that the candidate is happy for the interview to proceed.
7. Building a smooth bridge to the rest of the interview.

The interviewer himself will do more talking than in later phases.

Welcome and introductions

The best place to meet the candidate is the room where he is waiting; this is friendlier than arranging for him to be brought into the interview room by a secretary. It is welcoming for the chairman of a panel to go out, meet the candidate, bring him in and introduce him to the rest of the panel. In this way the building of rapport and a friendly atmosphere will have begun before the interview has started.

Conventional questions about the journey (provided it was not merely from the next street) may be appropriate.

Introductions should be informal, but include the name and

job title of all interviewers. If the panel is large, it is helpful to provide a name-plate in front of each member.

The introductions also provide an opportunity to make clear the degree of formality expected by using (or not using) first names.

The way interviewers approach the period of welcome is of paramount importance for the success of the interview. Inexperienced interviewers may make their mind up about the suitability of a candidate within the first minutes of an interview, and spend the remainder of the time seeking evidence to justify their belief. Some claim in so many words that the way a candidate walks into the room, or the way he shakes hands, tells all they want to know. But if our aim is to make the best selection, we must firmly hold back judgement until we have valid evidence.

Few questions are usually necessary at this stage. However, it may be helpful to check with internal candidates, or candidates at a second interview, that they do in fact know everyone present.

Introductory remarks

☐ **Hallo, my name is Malcolm Peel, I'm the Personnel Manager; I expect you remember getting a letter from me. This is Helen Green, our Chief Executive, and John Brown, the Computer Manager. Do you mind if we call you Fred?**

☐ **Good morning Mr Smith. My name is Peel, Personnel Manager. May I introduce Mrs Green, Chief Executive, and Mr Brown, Computer Manager. Please sit down.**

☐ **I think you know everyone?**

Establishing rapport

This stage can have a big effect on the success of the interview. Its length will depend on how quickly its objectives are achieved; with tense and nervous candidates more time will be needed than with confident candidates or those we already know.

An effective way of starting to build rapport is to pick out any person, place, organisation, school, college or leisure interest which the candidate and we both know. A club or regimental tie may help. It is surprising how often something can be found.

Whatever questions we ask during this stage must be easy – even pleasant – for the candidate to answer. Traps are likely to be counter-productive, and should not be used. Our interpret-ation of the replies will concentrate on deciding whether the candidate is sufficiently at ease to move to more important matters, although information may sometimes be picked up unexpectedly. If we *do* get an apparently important response, we must judge whether to probe it at once or later; usually it is wiser to wait until later.

Occasionally, it may be best to move on to the next phase rather than hang around artificially, as to do so can increase the tension. But if we do move on, we must be conscious of the need to get on to the right wavelength before we approach difficult areas or ask probing questions.

☐ 1. **How was your journey?**

R1. *No problem. Your map was a great help.*
R2. *The traffic was dreadful. I was stuck behind one of these juggernauts most of the way, and there was this fool in a red Orion who kept on trying to overtake on bends. In the end, he cut right in and nearly had me into a ditch ...*

Replies will usually be conventional and uninformative, as with R1.

Occasionally they may suggest that the candidate is either unduly tense about travel or does not travel much. This will normally only matter if the job involves much travelling, or if the question of daily commuting would arise if the candidate were appointed. In this case it will need probing at some stage.

☐ S. **How long did it take you?**

R1. *Not as long as I thought it might. The train only took 35 minutes, and it was an hour and a quarter door-to-door. Morning and evening, I reckon it would just about give me time to finish the crossword.*

If the candidate himself comments on the question of regular travelling, he has clearly taken his application seriously. If he does not, we will need to follow up later.

☐ 2. **I see you were at Much Binding Comprehensive. I was there from '70 to '75. How is Smithy getting on as Head?**

R1. *Spends most of the time looking through his telescope. Had a new comet or something named after him last year.* etc.

We will undertake fuller exploration of his time at school (if we need to) during the next stage. That is not our current objective, and purely conventional replies will be fine. Depending on how relaxed we judge the candidate to be, we may or may not prolong the chit-chat on this or any other subject about which he is happy to talk naturally.

☐ 3. **So you follow Barsetshire. I managed to get to Lord's for the Final last September. How do you rate their chances this season?**

R1. *Not so good, I'm afraid. I was with the lads down at the indoor school, and they were not at all happy now Jones has left. They were even joking about asking me back.*

This appears to suggest that the candidate might have had a career in professional sport. If so, this will give us an additional opportunity to explore his work motivation. The best move is probably to check whether our interpretation is correct straightaway, while the subject is with us.

☐ S. **Oh. I hadn't realised you played with them. Tell me about it.**

☐ 4. **I lived in Bolton for a couple of years in the sixties. What sort of a place is it to live in these days?**

R1. *You wouldn't recognise it. They've torn down all the old buildings and cut a huge new road right through the centre ...*

R2. *We love the place. It's my wife's home town, and she always says she would sooner leave me than it.*

Conventional replies such as R1 need no comment.

R2, on the other hand, appears to indicate a major relocation problem. Too quick a follow-up might bring a retraction. We must note carefully and follow up later.

The selection procedure

We should briefly explain the procedure we are using and how the present interview fits into it. We may also quickly outline the ground we intend the interview to cover, in what order, and approximately how long it should last.

This will help us to exercise control as the interview progresses. If the interviewee should move outside the defined area, or spend too long on a particular point, we can refer to this introductory statement, and bring the proceedings back on track.

□ 5. **We're holding first interviews this week: I'm seeing about 15 people. We plan to invite our short-listed candidates to meet the whole Board, probably at the start of next month. I expect we'll want to spend about an hour together this morning. I'll tell you something about us first, and the post we want to fill. Then, I'd like to learn about you. Finally, I expect you will have some questions to ask me. Is that OK?**

R1. *Yes, fine.*
R2. *Oh, I see. As a matter of fact, I've had a final interview for another job, and they said they'd let me know by Friday. Would there be any chance of speeding things up, or at least letting me know by Friday whether you want to take this one further?*

R1 calls for no comment.

R2 might suggest that the candidate is more interested in the other job, although this is by no means certain. It is usually best to probe such a situation at once.

□ S. **That could be difficult. Would you mind telling me about the other job?**

R1. *Not at all. It's with the Department of Technology ...*
R2. *If you don't mind, I'd prefer not to go into detail.*

Having raised the issue, most candidates will talk reasonably frankly about the other job. If they do, much may be learnt, especially from its similarities or differences from the current post, which should be probed if necessary.

R2 is difficult to interpret as it stands. This reaction may arise from general secrecy, fear of contact between the two employers, or perhaps because the application is to a trade rival.

On balance, R2 suggests that the other post is likely to be offered, and would be preferred. On the other hand, it may mean we are too near to calling a bluff.

In either case, the best hope of probing is probably to refer to the 'other job' towards the end of the interview, when the possibility of a second interview for this one may seem more real; occasionally, the 'other job' may have been forgotten by then.

If we wish to probe further now, we may try:

- □ S. **If they do make an offer, how will you react?** or
- □ S. **I doubt if our Board could get together any earlier. Would you be prepared to wait for their decision, or would you have to finalise the other offer immediately?**

R1. *That's no problem.*
R2. *I promised to let them know straightaway.*

In most cases, the reply will indicate reasonable flexibility, as with R1.

R2 is an attempt to pressurise us, and suggests a strong and confident candidate. If these characteristics are on the person profile, we will be keen to continue, and work round the difficulty later.

If not, we may decide that the implied deadline can only be resisted. If the candidate is prepared to keep to our reasonable time-scale, fine; if not, we can do nothing and are entitled to ask whether there is any point in continuing with the application.

Knowledge of the organisation

We must find out if the knowledge the candidate has of the job and the organisation is what we expect it to be. Has he seen the advertisement and received, read, understood and remembered the paperwork we have sent? Has he any additional source of information (such as friends or relatives)? If any important gaps are revealed, it will usually be necessary to repair them at once, so that the proceedings can start from the proper baseline.

Some recruiters use this as the first area of serious evaluation, on the basis that a worthwhile and serious candidate will not only have read and digested the job advertisement and any inform-ation sent to him, but will have researched the organisation from other sources.

□ 6. **What do you know about Green & Co (= us)?**

R1. *Only what it said in the ad. To tell the truth, I'd never heard of you before.*

R2. *Well, I know you make medical products, have sites here and in Harlow, employ about 1500 people, and are owned by a US parent. Not much more, I'm afraid.*

R3. *I looked you up in a couple of directories, and I was able to find a friend whose wife used to work for you. I discovered that ... (A detailed summary, from which the interviewer himself may learn a thing or two.)*

It is all too easy to be impressed by sound knowledge of our own operation, and upset by lack of it, especially if we are the proprietor or a senior executive. But we must keep a sense of perspective, and judge the reply strictly according to the person profile.

If the applicant lives in the same town or neighbourhood as the organisation, a poor answer such as R1 suggests a candidate lacking in real interest not only in our organisation, but in the world of work in general; it may be a serious negative.

If the situation involves the candidate in applications to different organisations, as in graduate recruitment, an efficient answer is an important indication of good faith in this specific application, and demonstrates that the applicant's thinking has got further than 'It's Tuesday, so this must be Green's'.

If the post is senior, a comprehensive answer such as R3 suggests a keen candidate, a serious application and an ability to research relevant data.

If the post is very senior (director or partner level), anything less than R3 must be a grave failing.

If, however, none of these factors applies, a poor answer may have little bearing on the suitability of the candidate; we must resist the desire for flattery.

Whatever view we take, it is necessary to fill the important gaps in the applicant's knowledge, but without overloading him; he will remember little of what is told him at this stage of an interview.

Knowledge of the post to be filled

Questioning in this area is essential, so that we can examine the candidate's understanding of what he has applied for, fill in any important gaps, and observe his reaction to the new knowledge. Before reaching this stage, he will normally have read an advertisement, and we may have let him have more detailed information before or while he was waiting for the interview. We may have given him a tour round the work area and introduced him to potential colleagues.

If he shows that he has not made proper use of the information he has been given, we must be right in marking him down. We will certainly wish to probe and if we are dissatisfied, we may even query whether the application is worth pursuing.

On the other hand, failure to understand the nature of the post may be the result of poor or misleading information from us. In this case, we will need to tread carefully, to supply the missing detail, and to enquire humbly whether that changes the candidate's view of the post.

As with information about the organisation, there is no point in overloading the candidate, who will not be in a fit state to take in a mass of detail. If we are in charge of the post, there is a real danger that we will hold forth too long.

This aspect of the selection *must* be two-way. The more accurately the candidate understands what is required, the more we can help each other towards a correct decision. Even if we have skeletons in the cupboard (poor working conditions, exceptional work load, inexperienced colleagues) he will find out if he joins us, when the shock may cause him to leave, or at least to continue in a disaffected and unco-operative frame of mind.

Selection consultants, in their role as honest brokers, will have an advantage here and will be able to make any necessary and helpful comments from a detached position.

This stage can form a natural bridge from the introduction to the subsequent phases of the interview.

☐ 7. **What do you know about this job?**

R1. *Well, nothing except the title and the salary; I hoped you would tell me.*

R2. *Only the details you sent me. As I understand it, it's based here, although there will be travel within the UK. It will be in charge of a section of five systems analysts. The work will be for a major new client, and involve a fully integrated prediction and stock control system. You require recent XYZ experience.*

R3. *I understand the title and the description you gave in the advertisement, which match my own expertise. But to be truthful, I found some aspects a little vague. My contacts tell me you are completing a big re-organisation of this area, so I imagine that is why. I'm sure you will fill in the detail for me.*

R1 is wet in the extreme. Unless there is some special factor (like an internal candidate who was instructed to apply for a newly created post) we may want to probe at once:

☐ S. **Then why did you apply?**

R2 is a sensible, standard reply, to which we may possibly want to add a few additional details.

R3 places the ball firmly in our court. It appears to be the reply of a worthwhile candidate who deserves an explanation if his remarks are justified. Over to us.

Following information we offer to any of the candidates, we would be wise to probe.

☐ S. **Is it what you expected when you applied, or have there been any surprises in what you have learnt?**

The reply to this may reveal the need for further information, or to correct misunderstanding. At worst, it may lead to a mutual parting of the ways.

Is all well?

At this stage, we should have cleared the ground, and be ready to move into the more testing phases of the interview. We should have established a reasonably easy relationship with the candidate, who should be talking with increasing freedom. We should have established what he knows about our organisation and the job he has applied for, and filled in any gaps. We should have started to get a feel for his personality and motivation in his working life. If there are any major problems, there is a reasonable chance we may already have brought them to the surface.

However, very occasionally, an interview may collapse at this point; either we or the candidate may discover that we have a fundamental misunderstanding about why we are together, and realise that the most sensible course is for us to face this and halt the proceedings without further waste of time.

Something may have weakened the candidate's interest in going further. We may doubt whether the candidate is on the right wavelength. Perhaps an important answer has been off-cue. Perhaps his body language appears to show undue anxiety. If this is the case, we need to find out now, and not go blindly into the next phase.

☐ 8. **Does all that make sense, or are there any other aspects you would like to clear up before we go on?**

Question 14 may perform the same function.

R1. *No, that's fine, thanks. Just what I had expected from the advertisement.*

R2. *I think so ... I wasn't completely clear whether you are prepared to appoint above the minimum of the salary range.*

R3. *Yes. I wasn't sure from what you said whether I would report to the marketing director or the sales manager. I already report to a director, and I wouldn't want to take a step down.*

R4. *Could you enlarge on what you said about the travelling? We have two young children, and I don't want to spend many nights away from home, at the present time.*

At this stage, the candidate is likely to be embarrassed in expressing serious problems, and may mention them, if at all, only indirectly. We are looking for something that sounds firm and convincing, like R1. Hesitation or double-takes in the answer may thus be significant. R2, R3 and R4 all display doubts, and cannot be passed over without probing. For R2, we may probe:

☐ S. **We hardly ever do that. Let me see; you're on 10k at the moment. We would start whoever we appointed on 10, which is the bottom of the range, as you know. Would this work for you, or what are you looking for?**

R1. *Well, I thought from the ad that you would pay anything within the range if you found the right candidate. Of course, the job's exactly what I'm after, but I'd have to travel further, and I don't want to take a drop.*

This sounds very negative. Such a candidate will probably pull out at some stage, so why waste each other's time? If we really can't pay above the minimum, the right course would probably be to face facts and terminate the interview now.

R3 and R4 need similar probes:

☐ **S. No, you would report to the sales manager. I wouldn't want there to be any doubt about that. From what you say, the post is clearly not what you had in mind?**

☐ **S. It would vary, of course; some weeks would be spent entirely in the office; occasionally, you might be away the whole week if, say, you were visiting our agents in Scotland. But the person who took this post would have to be prepared to average about two nights away each week. This does not sound as if it would be right for you?**

In each case, anything less than a convincing, credible acceptance of the position suggests we should both bite the bullet and terminate the interview now:

☐ **S. Well, that's how it is. I'm afraid we have no flexibility on this. In view of what you say, I think the wisest course is for us to face facts now, rather than waste any more of each other's time, and admit that this post is not for you. Do you agree?**

Building a smooth bridge

It is a common mistake to conclude the introductory phase with a pause, a change of tone, and something which sounds like (or even says in so many words) 'Right, we've played around long enough, now let's get down to business.' If we do this, we risk spoiling all we have done to relax the candidate, establish rapport, and get him talking freely.

The next phase will be an examination of the CV, and the smoothest bridge is therefore often to pick some relatively neutral aspect of the CV and ask a broad, not unduly demanding question. By using this, we can also begin to learn something of the candidate's personality and motivational system.

However, there are also traps for the interviewer in the use of this sort of question, and we must beware.

☐ 9. **How did you enjoy your time at St Trinian's?**

R1. *I had a great time. We were quite a good year, though I say it myself. All but three went on to Oxbridge, and the others went straight into their family businesses. We still meet up every year on Speech Day.*

R2. *It was OK, although the school was too large. The Head didn't know all the teachers, let alone pupils.*

R3. *I got good O levels, but my parents wouldn't let me stay on to the sixth. My dad was redundant by then, and mum wasn't very well.*

The importance of these replies will depend on how long ago it all was. It we are interviewing a school-leaver or a graduate, school-days will be vastly more important than with a 40-year-old; indeed they will be most of what we have to go on.

Most candidates will claim to have enjoyed school, but the words used may modify the picture. Even 40 years on, the filtered memory of schooldays will give us some indication of the priorities, the way important decisions are made and the general values and motivation of the candidate.

R1 emphasises achievement, and sounds like the reply of an ambitious, well-motivated person. Whether this is so, the rest of the CV and the interview will make clearer.

R2 tells us little. It may be lack of interest, poor memory, or deliberate defensiveness. Other answers will tell us which. If school is important, we will probe straightaway; if it is not, we will pass on and await later clues.

R3 is the classic bad luck story. It may be self-pity and a basis of excuses for later failure, or it may be a tale of a gritty rise by one's own bootstraps. Later developments will have special interest for us. We may decide to probe immediately.

☐ 10. **It's good to meet someone else who did National Service. What, looking back, do you feel you got from it?**

R1. *Not a lot. Blancoing belts and polishing boots is about all I can remember.*

R2. *Wonderful time. I'm certain that if we still had it, most of the problems with today's youth would disappear overnight. And it would help with unemployment.*

R3. *Mixed, I think. I did learn a lot about myself which I doubt I could have learnt without it. But a lot of the time was totally wasted. On the whole I envy today's young men able to start their career two years earlier.*

This can be dangerous ground. It opens up social, possibly political attitudes which may be held very strongly, by interviewer or interviewee.

The bad interviewer will award high marks to someone whose prejudices match his own. The good interviewer will be prepared to use such questions if he can rigidly exclude his own biases and preconceptions in judging the reply. If not, he will steer clear. The real value of the replies will lie in what they tell about the maturity and quality of thought of the candidate.

R1 appears superficial, and suggests a candidate who does not take a serious view either of his own experience or of social issues. We will watch to see whether other replies reinforce or cancel out this impression.

As far as it goes, R2 also shows little evidence of clear thinking, although the view may have been the result of careful thought. We must avoid prejudice, and watch for evidence from less highly charged subjects.

R3 appears to indicate mature and sensible analysis, which again needs checking as the interview proceeds.

☐ 11. **Traditional apprenticeships seem to be on the way out. What do you think of this change, based on your own time as a craft apprentice?**

R1 *I think it's a mistake. Five years is a long time, sure, but no exam could test all you learnt in that time. You learn with your hands more than these fancy college boys will ever know.*

R2. *It had to come. All these restrictive practices were wrecking the industry.*

R3. *YTS are just sweated labour. The bosses just wanted an excuse to cut wages.*

Here also, the danger of warming to political biases that match our own is obvious, and the question is, for that reason, dangerous. However, like question 21, it can, with care, be legitimately used to assess the quality and maturity of thought.

To do so, we will need to probe each reply further, and avoid, in doing so, getting drawn into controversy.

5
THE CV: TIMES PAST

Overall objectives

1. To fill any factual gaps in the CV and probe any doubtful areas.
2. To learn about past behaviour which may help to predict behaviour in the post to be filled.
3. To explore technical competence.

Using the CV in date order provides a sequence for questioning which has a logic for both candidate and interviewer. It provides a natural order and a built-in memory jogger. It becomes easier for the candidate to explain and for the interviewer to understand the way events have unrolled and the pattern they have formed. It also provides a built-in checklist to ensure nothing of importance is forgotten.

This approach also recognises that the best predictor of future behaviour is past behaviour, when correctly understood and interpreted. This is not to say that we will act in the same way next time; the action we took may not have worked. Nothing can predict human reactions with certainty, but the past is usually the best guide available.

In using the CV in this way, we will need to keep a sense of perspective. Some areas we will pass over quickly; we may not explore O-level grades, for example, when interviewing a 40-year-old PhD. But other areas may prove of unexpected importance; we may spend a good deal of time on the reasons why a particular project failed if we detect close similarity with a major element in the present job.

This phase will usually form an excellent framework for the

entire central section of the interview, into which exploration of technical competence, personality factors, relevant circumstances and the longer-term future will all be fitted.

(Needless to say, this must *not* be the first time we have studied the CV. For effective selection we should have done this at least twice before; once when making up the list for interview, and once when preparing before the interviews themselves.)

Filling in the gaps

Any gap may suggest some bending of the story, and filling it may reveal something relevant. However, we have no time to waste; we must tread a path between naive trust and small-minded suspicion, but human nature being what it is, it is usually safer to err on the side of suspicion.

Gap filling will go on at the same time as we are engaged on other aspects of this phase.

☐ 1. **You don't say what you were doing after leaving Black's in July 1980 until you joined White's in April '81?**

R1. *I wasn't at all sure what I wanted to make of things, so I tried one or two temporary jobs.*

R2. *No, actually I was job hunting then.*

R3. *I was self-employed.*

R4. *Oh, didn't I put that in? I worked as a bus driver in Liverpool.*

Any time gap in a CV must raise suspicions that something is being hidden. The candidate may have been:

- in a job that doesn't fit the rest of his CV
- in a job from which he was dismissed
- unemployed
- in hospital, perhaps with a mental condition
- in gaol.

The possibility of someone actually forgetting what they were doing is remote, especially as the fact that a gap is shown indicates the period itself has been remembered. But before jumping to the more extreme conclusions, it is sensible to find out whether it is a simple oversight in completing the paperwork.

Whatever answer is given is almost certain to need probing, but in doing so we must avoid sounding inquisitorial. We may remind ourselves of the mistakes we may have made in our own career, and of the fact that the mental hospital and the gaol are places from which society aims to send people out as fully restored members of society. We are not judges; we simply need to know.

R1 has a good chance of being correct, but we will need to probe:

- ☐ S. **What actually were the temporary jobs, and who were they with?** (Writing down the answers as given will concentrate the interviewee's mind.)
- ☐ S. **What went wrong?** (Of each in turn.)

R2 could mean anything. There is nothing wrong with job hunting, particularly in times of massive unemployment, but such a situation suggests that departure from the previous job was forced. We may try a succession of probes:

- ☐ S. **Why did you leave your previous job, if you had nothing lined up?**
- ☐ S. **What sort of jobs were you applying for, and how many applications did you make?**
- ☐ S. **What seemed to hold you back from getting any of them?**

If the statement is true, we will learn a good deal of relevance to the present situation.

Probes for R3 may be:

- ☐ S. **What did you hope for when you started the enterprise?**
- ☐ S. **How did it go, and what went wrong in the end?**

It will be easier to be satisfied of the truth of this statement than the others, as self-employment is usually a matter of pride, even if it goes wrong. It will certainly tell a great deal about the interviewee.

R4 sounds convincing, but should be probed:

- ☐ S. **That's an interesting move; why did you do that?**
- ☐ S. **What made you leave your job?**
- ☐ S. **Why, as a matter of interest, didn't you mention it in your CV?**

- ☐ 2. **You say you got an honours degree, but not which class.**

R1. *Sorry; it was a third.*
R2. *Second class.*

R1 sets the record straight, and without too much damage.

R2 does not. The difference between the classes of degree is significant, as every graduate knows. Not to state which raises the suspicion of a deliberate piece of wool-pulling. It requires the follow-up:

□ S. **Upper or lower?**

The need for us to press this so hard must leave a doubt as to the openness of the candidate.

□ 3. **What salary were you on when you finally left White's?**

R1. *£8750.*
R2. *I'm not sure. I think it was about 9k.*

This is another significant point, which may put the less than frank candidate in a spot. We should probe a reply such as R2.

□ S. **Oh. Can you be more specific?**

Too high a figure may raise the question of why he left for whatever his next starting salary was; too low a figure the question of why his employers did so little to reward and keep him.

Relating past to future

To try to project the candidate's future behaviour from how he has behaved in the past is the centre of the interview. There is much we could ask, and we will need to choose with care.

□ 4. **Why did you decide to go into computing when you got your degree?**

R1. *Most of my friends were doing the same thing. IBZ came on the milkround, and gave us very impressive interviews. The prospects looked fabulous.*
R2. *Well, a classics degree doesn't really lead anywhere directly. I looked round a bit and this was first to come up.*
R3. *I'd been interested in computing since my dad got a micro when I was about 13. I worked in XYZ in both my long vacs,*

the first operating on shifts, and the second on a big software project they had on.

The reasons for a graduate's first job choice may be far less clear than might be supposed. The majority of students study a subject because they are good at it, occasionally because they prefer certain teachers. It is unusual to choose degree subjects because they may lead to a particular career.

None of these replies need be seen as unfavourable, although R3 is clearly the most convincing and suggests a lively mind fully switched on to the chosen career.

R1 and R2 will probably need follow-up.

□ S. **How do you feel about the choice now?**

□ 5. **What made you leave White's after 10 years with them?**

R1. *They had just lost a couple of their biggest clients, and things didn't look good. There was a lot of talk of redundancies in the offing.*

R2. *I couldn't see any chance of more promotion. My boss was younger than me, and his boss had only been in a year, and looked set to stay a long while.*

R3. *Black's were advertising for people with just my background, but at 3k a year more than I was getting.*

R4. *I was made redundant.*

R5. *I had a flaming row with my boss.*

R6. *They asked me to resign.*

A change of employer in mid-career is still a cause of suspicion to some. They may feel that to leave after about a decade of service with one employer demonstrates failure. By that time a person's potential should be fully known, and if he is failing to get promotion that satisfies him, his self-image is unrealistic. Other recruiters would not share this view, but most would feel that a change after such a period does merit an explanation.

R1 could be just such a reasonable explanation, but is worth a probe:

□ S. **What happened to the firm, in the end?**

R2 may also be perfectly valid. Careers easily get gummed up in their middle years through no fault of their owner. But a probe is justified.

☐ S. **How did your prospects start to get fouled up?**

R3 likewise may be fine. The probe might be:

☐ S. **How much more did you get, in the event?**

R4 must be probed. 'Redundancy' may mean several things, from a well-compensated, mass event to a polite synonym for an individual sacking. Occasionally, with longer serving employees, even the person involved may not realise the full implications of what was done to them. Follow-ups might begin:

☐ S.   **Can you tell me more about the exact circumstances of your redundancy?**

This may be followed by more detailed probes.

R5 has the great merits of being refreshingly direct and apparently honest. R6 is a real pre-emptive strike. Both clearly invite follow-up, and for that reason the wily and suspicious interviewer may look beneath the surface.

☐ S. **Go on; please tell me the gory detail.**

☐ 6. **Tell me about your relationship with your boss during this phase.**

R1. *Just ordinary. No problems.*
R2. *He was an interesting character. In many ways the best I've worked for, but in some ways he could be a little difficult.*
R3. *I found him impossible. He took all the credit, and passed on all the blame. He was one of the main reasons I left.*
R4. *A great guy. Working with him was better than studying for an MBA (Master of Business Administration degree). I learnt most of what I know from him.*

Attitude towards our boss is one of the more transferable of work behaviours. It often reflects deep-seated views of authority in general, perhaps based on the parent-figures of early life. If we can learn anything of the candidate's attitude to past bosses, we have a sporting chance of learning how he would view us if we inherited the role.

Boss-attitude can also be a good indicator of the kind of job satisfaction the candidate hopes for.

R1 is defensive and non-committal. We may try a couple of probes, to establish whether it is a deliberate response, or just a weak answer.

☐ S. **How good was he to work for?**

☐ S. **What problems did you find working for him?**

R2 is diplomatically phrased, but tends towards the negative. It invites follow-up, although as always the response must not automatically be taken at face value.

☐ S. **Tell me more.**

R3 may be an honest statement of fact, or sour grapes. The candidate himself, being involved in the situation, may not be able to disentangle the whole truth. We must at least try.

☐ S. **That is very sad. Can you give me one or two instances?**

R4 sounds absolutely super; a healthy, outgoing and honest response which augurs well for future bosses. If it is not, our chances of cracking it are slim. All we can do is note it and compare for consistency with other replies.

☐ 7. **What do you feel was your most worthwhile achievement at Brown's, and why?**

R1. *Well, there were a lot really. Nothing very specific, but keeping the job going was an achievement, you know.*

R2. *Oh, sorting out the Borneo assignment. The Japanese were after it. That was worth about £2m, plus follow-up business.*

R3. *There was no chance of any achievements. The job just didn't give the scope; that was why I left.*

R4. *Well-motivated and trained staff. That was my best achievement.*

Sound answers to this question can tell a great deal about the candidate's quality of work and motivational systems.

R1 sounds vague and wishy-washy, the answer of a low-quality candidate. We may try a probe by repeating the question in different words:

☐ S. **Did you do anything you were particularly proud of?**

Failing that, we will probably pass on discouraged.
R2 should be the good one, specific and testable. We can probe:

☐ S. **Great. Tell me about it?**

R3 is the ultimate negative. But the negative may reflect on the job, the candidate, or an unfortunate combination of the two. We must try to find out which.

☐ S. **What exactly held you back?**

R4 sounds suspiciously like a cop-out. It may be real, it may be a play for time, or it may be the only thing the interviewee can think of. We must probe:

☐ S. **Yes, of course. What, under your guidance, was your staff's finest achievement?**

☐ 8. **What problems did you meet when they first made you a supervisor, and how did you cope with them?**

R1. *Not a lot, really. It all worked out smoothly.*
R2. *I found it quite difficult, especially as they gave me no training. The worst was sorting out the lengthy tea breaks everyone took. I had to threaten one guy with the sack; right through the procedure to final warning before he came round.*
R3. *Budgeting was a bit of a headache. It wasn't just me; no one seemed to understand it.*

People are naturally loath to admit to difficulties at interview, even when invited to say how they overcame them.

R1 is evasive and sounds weak and is likely to be the reply of a weaker candidate. Probing might help something to the surface, but probably won't.

R2 sounds specific and frank, and gives an indication of a genuine problem faced and solved.

R3 is weak as it stands, suggesting an unresolved problem and a confused approach. We must probe:

☐ S. **How did you sort it out, finally?**

The reply to this may need further detailed probing.

□ 9. **Why did you take the post at Yellowlease College?**

R1. *It was what I had always wanted. I felt there was a really worthwhile job to be done with those young people, and I knew by then I had got the experience to help them.*

R2. *It was an opportunity to broaden my experience. This was a job at the right level, and it paid very well.*

R3. *I'd exhausted what Brown's had to offer, and I was ready to move on.*

The reasons for previous job moves should be informative, suggesting the sort of approach the candidate may be taking to the present application. Somehow this rarely works out so clearly at interview. If there is a good rise in salary, the candidate will probably feel the reasons are self-evident, although he will rarely say so in so many words. Often a probe produces more information than the original question.

R1 sounds positive and clear. The motivation is specific and forward looking and has a good moral tone to it, combining interest in the job with interest in people. We can follow up:

□ S. **How did it work out once you got there?**

R2 is the vague one, saying virtually nothing except that the new job paid better.

R3 looks backwards, not even mentioning the new job or employer. A probe for both this and R2 might be:

□ S. **What are your feelings about the move, looking back from where you are now?**

□ 10. **Looking back on your career so far, how does it match your hopes when you started, and how do you feel about the way it has worked out?**

R1. *It's strange how things happen. When I started, I intended to make a career in retailing, but the opportunities were never there. I've given up trying to plan the future now. I don't think it's worked out too badly, despite the changes.*

R2. *Not as well as I'd hoped, but then youth always is impatient. I wasted two good years at Brown's, although that was the children really, so I suppose they were not wasted. Then*

> *came the recession of '80–83. But I've got back on the road
> since then.*

R3. *I qualified as a chemist, and chemistry was what I wanted
to do. But in those days I didn't realise how limited the
opportunities for specialists are. I was hesitant about
moving into management, but now I've done it, I know I've
found my feet. Compared with management, chemistry was
narrow and dull.*

R4. *Bang on target. When I left school, I promised myself I would
take five years to look round, five years to build a base, and
then go for it. That's just what I've done, and now I'm ready
to start motoring.*

This question only makes sense with candidates who have been
around for a few years, but with such people it can tell a lot. They
may not have thought this way before, and replies may be
surprisingly frank.

R1 is rather sad. Clearly as a career, it's a big disappointment.
Such a candidate sounds most unlikely to pull up any trees, but
this may not be what we're looking for.

R2 sounds a sensible appreciation. Its failing is its lack of
reference to the work itself; 'on the road' sounds simply as if it's
the road to a higher salary.

R3 inspires a lot of confidence. It is specific, well expressed
and covers both work content and personal growth. By impli-
cation it looks forward to the next move.

R4 gives the impression of meaningless flannel. The best that
can be said is that it is crisp and confident. We may have such
qualities on our person profile.

□ 11. **What has been the most satisfying achievement in your
career to date?**

R1. *Keeping my first boss happy. He was someone no one else
could get on with.*

R2. *Almost chance really. It was when I was in the labs, and
suddenly came up with an answer to the corrosion problem
our main model was experiencing in tropical conditions.*

R3. *Landing the Scandinavian contract. It was worth over
£1m, and it took me nine months and eight visits to
Stockholm.*

R1 may or may not contain hidden gold, but the chances seem slim, from the way the reply is phrased. We must probe:

☐ S. **How did you do that?**

R2 may be spoilt for our present purpose by the 'chance' aspect, but much may depend on how readily others accepted the discovery.

☐ S. **How did the powers that be take your discovery?**

R3 seems to paint the picture we are looking for; a clear target and much hard work before it was at length attained. A simple request for more detail may be worthwhile.

☐ 12. **Tell me about the worst disagreement you have experienced during your career, and what came of it.**

R1. *I don't think I can remember any bad ones.*

R2. *I had a problem with one of the district reps once on the phone. He couldn't understand, or made out he couldn't, what I was telling him. In the end I slammed the phone down on him. He told his boss, who told mine, who tore into me. I still feel a bit sore about it, but I expect I was in the wrong really.*

R3. *There was a chap in the drawing office, and for some reason we hated each other's guts. No idea why – body chemistry or something. The trouble was, we had to work together, to see each other every day. I tried all I knew, short of shooting the guy, but he didn't want to know. Then one day I happened to walk into the office carrying a copy of the* Railway Magazine *I'd bought. That did it; he's been my closest pal at the place for a couple of years now.*

R1 is another conversation stopper; there seems little point in attempting a probe or supplementary question.

R2 and R3 both suggest reasonable insight into the candidate's relationships, and apparent honesty. On balance, R3 seems to be the story of someone with nothing to hide in this area of personality, and sounds like a one-off, while R2 just might be the tip of an iceberg, possibly even a muted call for help.

Technical competence

Surprisingly, technical competence can be a problem in selection. Several things may go wrong.

Different perspectives

Technical competence may be played up too much, on the assumption that a technical expert has everything, or nearly everything, that matters. On the other hand, it may be played down too much, in the belief that the necessary technical expertise can be learnt, but the right personality cannot. These differing perspectives may become a point of controversy between selectors.

Failure to assess

Technical competence may remain unassessed, even by those who are convinced that it matters.

The assumption may be made that it is guaranteed by claimed qualifications or previous experience. It may be felt that there is no meaningful way it can be assessed during the selection process. Non-technical selectors will usually be chary of trying to assess technical factors. Even those with technical knowledge may be hesitant, fearing perhaps that their knowledge may be out of date, that an interviewee may know more than they do, or even that it is ungentlemanly to doubt or question a fellow professional's knowledge.

Occasionally, exploring technical competence may fall between the stools of the different panel members or different interviews, everyone assuming that the others have assessed or will assess it.

The need to assess

The need to assess technical competence will depend on what the person profile requires, but there are few jobs in which it does not figure. However, the interview may not always be the only vehicle for assessment; performance tests and references may have a part to play.

The non-expert

The questions asked by the expert *as an expert* are outside the scope of this book, as they will be specific to each area of expertise.

There is no way that, as laymen, we can legitimately test knowledge and skills. If we tried to do so, using superficial acquaintance with a subject or questions suggested by someone else, we would be courting ridicule and disaster, and would not have the means of either controlling or evaluating what was said.

However, a non-expert can legitimately attempt to build up a picture of what the candidate believes to be his skills, how he has used them, and the confidence he has in them, all of which is useful, though incomplete date.

☐ 13. **What have you done since you first qualified to keep your knowledge up to date?**

R1. *Little outside my job. But I find that is very effective in itself.*

R2. *That was rather a long time ago, of course. I read quite a bit; journals, papers and so on. White's sent me on a couple of courses last year.*

R3. *I choose a course of some sort every year. This year I've started with the Open University, although to be honest I'm finding it a bit of a struggle so far, particularly with the children so young.*

Attitudes towards skill updating vary enormously, as do individual circumstances and opportunities.

This is an area in which our own views may cloud our judgement. If we are keen on education, training and obtaining qualifications for ourselves and those who work with us, we may be too insistent with those having different needs. The operative factors are ambition, age, and the rate of technical obsolescence in the relevant area.

R1 is very relaxed, and inappropriate either for a younger person who wants to get on or an older person in a rapidly changing environment. It is hardly an inspiring reply, except perhaps from the lips of a hard-working research scientist.

R2 may be a sensible attitude from someone in mid-career with heavy family responsibilities. The attitude should be probed, however.

☐ S. **Do you feel there is a danger of personal obsolescence? Might you be missing out?**

R3 sounds great, and just right from an ambitious younger person. We shall want to know what the 'courses' were, however, and what subjects are being studied through the Open University.

□ **14. What are the three most important skills that you have developed in your career so far?**

R1. *Number one is easy; keeping on the right side of the boss. Number two; well, I suppose the skill of prioritising work. Comes to the same thing, really, I suppose, ha ha. As for number three; I think I've developed a nose for the oddball, to mix metaphors; an instinct for something out of place – something that might go badly wrong (or sometimes right).*
R2. *Problem-solving, getting information out of other people, and keeping my head down.*
R3. *I've learnt how people matter more than facts, and a bit about how to handle them. I think I communicate well with almost everyone I work with, whatever level. I'm sure I have learnt how to sift out the irrelevant and remember the facts that really matter.*
R4. *I have become thoroughly computer-literate. I've learnt how to sell ideas, and I think I can weigh up people.*

The typical answers to this kind of question tend to home on to the 'soft' areas such as people skills, rather than the 'hard' areas of work skill. R4 mentions computer-literacy, but there is little to choose among the others.

Nevertheless, the question can be useful, as many of the items listed can be made the subject of a probe that will enter the area of job skills in some depth.

□ S. **Tell me how you go about prioritising your work.**
□ S. **Tell me of one or two problems you have faced and how you solved them.**
□ S. **What sort of facts do really matter in your present job?**
□ S. **How do you use your computer-literacy in what you do now?**

□ 15. **White's have quite a reputation in this kind of work.**

From your time with them, what, without giving away secrets, do they do better than the rest of us?

R1. *They certainly set very high standards. Everyone gets at least a week's training before they are allowed to touch an assignment, and we have regular team training half-days every month.*

R2. *I'm not sure there's anything really. It's difficult to judge from inside.*

R3. *They probably have more people on the job than other firms. We have six in our section, with only 100 clients between us.*

R4. *I think they are better than many, if I can say that without offence. Their systems were set up originally by old White himself, but every two years a consultant updates them. They're all set out in a magnificent manual, which is our holy bible. I guess I'd better not say much more, though.*

R2 is trivial, and suggests a trivial approach.

Both R1 and R4 sound meaty; R1 is open to probing, which should reveal useful information about the nature and level of the candidate's skills.

□ S. **What subjects would be covered in a typical training session?**

R4 has, accepting our invitation, carefully shut out the possibility of a probe, and we must leave it there.

R3 sounds of doubtful worth, but is wide open to detailed probing and comparison, which will help to show whether the impression of a possibly inadequate level of technical competence is justified.

□ S. **We have five for about 100 clients. But our section is responsible from first enquiry to debt collection. Which stages do your people cover?**

6
THE PRESENT: THE JOB

Overall objectives

1. To explore the scope and responsibilities of the candidate's present post (if any; if not, his most recent).
2. To match what he has to offer with the needs of the post to be filled.
3. To learn his expectations in regard to pay and conditions.

This phase consists of bringing up to date the exploration of the CV which was started in the previous phase, and relating it to the current vacancy.

The scope and responsibilities of the candidate's present or most recent post

Few people, especially in professional and more senior positions, move at random from one area or kind of work to another. Therefore, unless something has gone badly wrong, there will be a close relationship between the job the candidate is now doing and the job he may reasonably hope to do next. Some people do make step changes, or revert successfully to a previous phase of their career. But even in such cases, the present situation will be of great importance, if only to indicate what is being rejected and why.

Our approach to satisfactions and successes, failures and problems in our present job will show much about our skills and personality.

☐ 1. **Tell me what your responsibilties are in your present job.**

R1. *Well, I'm called administration officer. I do the paperwork for all the meetings, and report to the directors each month on how things are going.*

R2. *I have four main tasks; to service the management committee, and act as the point of liaison between it and the rest of the organisation; to manage the MD's private office; to control the strategic planning section; and to organise the annual conference. A mixed bag certainly, but full of fun.*

R3. *My main job is to make sure that the Old Man knows what's going on, and to keep people sweet. I'm his eyes and ears, especially as far as the senior management is concerned.*

R4. *I spend most of my time trying to see into the future. We like to think we have some of the best long-range planners in the country. I also pull in a number of bits and pieces no one else wants, like the annual conference.*

The way someone describes the responsibilities of his present post may be an indicator of how he approaches it and his success in it. The aspects he chooses to emphasise, those he does not mention, and the general shape and clarity of his reply can tell us a good deal.

However, there are two important caveats. First, the more articulate will naturally explain better than the less articulate, and we must remember how prominently this skill figures in our person profile; we may not be looking for this. Second, this is an easy question to foresee and plan for. The probes may reveal more than the original question.

R1 sounds poor for what must be seen as a high-level post. Unless the candidate is still unduly nervous, or there are other special reasons, we may well doubt the quality of his work.

R2, on the other hand, is particularly crisp and well balanced. If supported by other evidence, it suggests someone with a good grasp of his job.

R3 and R4 offer very different views of the same post. R3 emphasises the communication and human relationship aspects, while R4 concentrates on the sophistication of the long-range planning job to the open disparagement of his other responsibilities. The likelihood in both cases must be that the neglected areas are outside the candidate's interests and probably his skills also.

☐ 2. **Can you explain to me how your present post fits into the structure of your organisation?**

R1. *I work for the personnel director basically. I organise the management training courses for the division and keep our instructors up to scratch.*

R2. *I report to the site director, although I also have a functional line to the company training manager. I have a staff of eleven; five instructors, two office staff, my secretary, one technician and two cleaners.*

R3. *I'm responsible for all management development activities within the division, answerable to the managing director.*

Many candidates feel an understandable need to exaggerate their importance within their organisation. The commonest way of doing this is to blur reporting lines, perhaps by forgetting layers above them, or making the indirect responsibilities of colleagues sound like a boss/subordinate relationship.

R1 sounds as if it is doing this. We will certainly need to probe:

☐ S. **Could you sketch the structure within your area, please, to show me just how everyone relates?**

R2 appears precise and understandable, and if it is consistent with other information, we cannot ask for more.

R3 is particularly vague, to the point of deliberate evasion. We may probe with question 3 and also be inclined to view other replies with a degree of suspicion.

☐ 3. **How is your effectiveness in your present post measured?**

R1. *Well, er, we all have budgets and things. I suppose the best indication is lack of complaints. People soon complain if things go wrong.*

R2. *It's measured at annual appraisal. We have objectives which are recorded and reviewed each year. It isn't a very effective system, to tell the truth. Feedback from my boss and my colleagues is the best measure I have.*

R3. *The principal measure is the budget. I have both a cost and a revenue budget, for which I am fully accountable. The bottom line is what counts most. Apart from this, I have a great deal of freedom to make my own mistakes.*

R4. *I like to set myself the highest standards. I monitor our delivery performance weekly, and also the monthly sales of every item. I record every complaint, and personally check the cause and the action taken.*

Failure to answer this question impressively must not always be laid at the door of the candidate. In many cases, a poor answer may also be a truthful one, and the fault of the candidate's boss or his organisation rather than himself.

However, few effective employees will sound happy if their work is inadequately evaluated, and the reaction of the candidate to the situation is often more significant than the situation itself.

R1 sounds as if the candidate hasn't even thought about the subject before and appears weak.

R2 gives the impression of someone struggling under a poor system, without achieving much success.

R3 is crisp and clear. It is good if supported by other evidence, but if we have doubts, we will need to probe:

☐ S. **How often do you meet your boss, and what do you discuss when you meet?**

R4 appears very positive; someone who feels the need to monitor his own work closely, probably in the absence of effective external control. We will probably want to probe this:

☐ S. **How do your boss and the organisation monitor your success?**

☐ 4. **Tell me of a recent project, explaining what aspects gave you most satisfaction.**

R1. *That's the snag with my present job. It gives me hardly any scope to make my own decisions.*

R2. *They asked me to re-organise the export documentation. I read up on O&M (organisation and methods) and studied it in depth. I identified 15 ways we could improve it, which saved over £10,000 a year, and made it over two days*

> *quicker. My boss said the report was the best he'd seen for*
> *years, and gave a copy of it to his director.*

R3. *I changed the way we purchase office supplies. It took me*
nearly a year. I fell foul of the office services manager, and
it turned out later that the previous supplier was a golfing
friend of the MD. But I got it through in the end, and saved
nearly £5000.

It is not enough to plan carefully, to achieve good interpersonal relations or effective communications. The ultimate test of success is to get where we want to be.

R1 is sad. There are many jobs without enough scope, but few in which someone with real drive cannot achieve at least some of what he believes to be right.

Depending on the view other answers have given of the candidate, we may feel a supplementary question is worthwhile:

☐ S. **What decisions would you like to have taken?**

R2 clearly describes an interesting assignment, which probably demonstrates a number of valuable skills. But there is a notable lack of reference to actual change, and the amount of drive it demonstrates will probably depend on the answer to a probe such as:

☐ S. **How many of your recommendations have actually been implemented?**

R3 sounds good; an honest description of difficulties overcome. But in case of 'flannel', a probe will make the situation even clearer:

☐ S. **How did you manage it?**

☐ 5. **What problems have you met in relationships with your present colleagues, and what techniques have you developed to overcome them?**

R1. *None, really. We're on very good terms.*

R2. *I suppose the biggest problems were with the warehouse*
people. They're not the highest calibre of staff down there,
and communication can be a problem. In the end, I've
found writing memos the best. You can prove what you told
them that way.

R3. *Maybe I shouldn't say it, but I found problems getting on the best terms with some of the female supervisors. They're a race I don't understand very well, and they certainly don't seem to understand me. I haven't altogether cracked the problem yet, but I think I'm making progress, slowly.*

We are likely to get no more from trying to probe R1 than we already have. Best to admit defeat on that one and try another.

R2 gives the clear impression of an arrogant person with a lot to learn. If we ask him:

□ **How do you get on with your superiors?**

and he answers:

R1. *Oh, no problem there.*

this impression will be confirmed.

R3 is frank and specific. While one failing is admitted, the impression is left that other relationships are good.

□ 6. **Why do you want to leave your present post?**

R1. *Well, I find the work boring now, and of course Black's don't pay well ...*

R2. *Career progression. I've been at Black's for three years now, and the time has come to make a move before I freeze to the spot.*

R3. *In many ways I'm very happy where I am; I'm not looking around actively. But the post you are filling seems to me the chance of a lifetime; it calls for the skills I have and offers the scope I want.*

R4. *My boss and I have fallen out. Life has been tough for a while, but now it's become impossible.*

This is as near a compulsory question as any on the list, but for that reason it is easy to anticipate and prepare for, and may tell us little. To be of value, the replies will need comparison with our other data. We may decide that question 7 offers more mileage.

R1 is weak and negative. The most charitable interpretation must be that the candidate has prepared badly.

R2 is not a lot better; it says nothing positive, and may hide negative reasons.

R3 sounds a good reply. It denies problems in the present post, while emphasising the closeness of fit with the post we are filling. However, to be convincing, what it says must match up with the other data we have.

R4 appears startlingly frank, and may be the reply of a good candidate. On the other hand, it may be a pre-emptive strike designed to defend a dodgy problem, such as just having been fired. To find out which, we must probe now, and compare with our other data:

☐ S. **Now there's a thing. Please tell me more.**

The match with what the candidate has to offer

We will already have started to form our own opinions about this, but it will help if we can discuss it openly with the candidate.

☐ 7. **Why have you applied for this job?**

R1. *My present job gives me no chance to use my education and skills. The company has no idea how to use graduates. I have a lot more to offer, and I want the chance to do so.*

R2. *To tell the truth, my boss and I don't see eye to eye. We haven't quite got to the point of no return, but we soon will. I want out, quickly.*

R3. *From the advertisement, it is exactly what I'm looking for, and I'm exactly what you're looking for. Your organisation makes a fine product. I can offer top professionalism. Together we will make a winning team. Oh yes, and there's the money.*

R4. *The job you describe is one I understand thoroughly, enjoy, and know I can do well. My knowledge of your organisation, from my contacts and from what I have read, tells me it is somewhere I would fit in particularly well. It would give me a chance to contribute, and to grow with the job.*

This is the converse of question 6. If the reply to that does not cover this area, we may follow up with question 7 immediately. We may prefer to use this question instead of question 6.

It is an area in which the honesty of the interviewer is as much on trial as that of the candidate. We all like to be told how good we, our job and our organisation are. But if we face facts, we must know that people apply for jobs for both negative and positive reasons.

The negative reasons arise from discontent with the present situation (be it job or unemployment). Indeed, unless the applicant feels this, why should he go through the trauma of a job move? We may feel that some kinds of discontent ('lack of scope', 'poor prospects', 'no opportunity to use my skills' etc) are more acceptable than others ('I've fallen out with my boss', 'I've got myself into the wrong kind of work', 'I don't enjoy what I'm being asked to do'). But at the end of the day, these may all turn out to mask similar situations.

The positive reasons, if honestly stated, almost always begin with the chance to be paid more, but interviewers conventionally tend to mark down those who admit this too readily. Most candidates will have rehearsed the line they judge best.

We should try not to use this question as a means of getting strokes and compliments, and look carefully behind whatever form of words is used.

R1 conveys a touch of arrogance. Few organisations use new graduates as they would like to be used; our own may disappoint this candidate in the same way. It is worth checking whether this is his first job since graduating; if not, the prognosis looks bleak. Other factors in our assessment will be the length of time he has held the job, and whether it includes, or is intended to include, an element of training. The transition from student to employee can be hard in the most favourable circumstances.

R2 stands out badly, being entirely backward looking and negative. It does not glance once at the post on offer. But we could be wrong to reject a candidate simply because he is so frank about a problem that most of us have experienced. We should probe:

□ S. **I understand how you feel about your present situation. But are you just applying for anything to get away, and if not, why did you choose this job?**

R3 is brash in the extreme, and sounds as if it has been learnt from a book on how to succeed at interview. A back answer from us may help the candidate to do himself justice:

□ S. **You sound more like a salesman than a person. Would you like to try again, speaking as you might to an intelligent friend?**

R4 says all the right things in just about the right way. We must note and compare with the other replies, such as those to the next two questions, before final acceptance as valid evidence.

☐ 8. **What do you believe you can offer that the post needs?**

R1. *I've done quite a few of the jobs before, over the years. I would need to learn the way you do things, of course, but so would anyone.*

R2. *I've got enthusiasm and drive. I'm a good team person. I learn fast. I'm loyal, hard-working and well motivated.*

R3. *Everything, from what you say. I'm doing a very similar technical job now, and the customer contact I did in my previous job. Apart from the new documentation, I could sit down and get on with it now.*

R4. *I know about polymers both in theory, from my HND (Higher National Diploma), and in practice, from my time in the Baxo Labs. I work with clients now and have a good track record in solving their problems. I'm a self-starter and I think I can show I'm creative.*

Some of the detail needed to substantiate these answers may have been covered by other questions. The probes below and comments on lack of substantiation assume that this has not happened. The aspect of qualifications may be covered in the reply; if not, we may use question 9 in addition.

R1 sounds unenthusiastic and, if the candidate can express no greater confidence in such an important matter, it is difficult for us to feel any on his behalf.

R2 is full of the most general words which, apart from making unsubstantiated claims, could be trotted out whatever the job. One doubts whether this candidate has even understood what we need.

R3 offers no proof for its claims, and we must probe before judging.

☐ S. **It would be interesting to try, but sadly that can't be arranged. Will you give me a rather more detailed list of the similarities between this and your present job?**

R4 does rather better at offering detail, but would still benefit from probing:

☐ S. **Please give me, very briefly, a couple of instances of the problems you've solved for customers.**

□ 9. **Which of your qualifications do you see as relevant to this post, and how?**

R1. *Well, naturally, my BSc (Bachelor of Science degree) in Computer Science, my membership of the British Computer Society and, as it's a management job, my Diploma in Management Studies and my membership of the British Institute of Management.*

R2. *I think my degree in English is relevant; of course, the subject isn't, but the mental discipline and critical attention to detail is. I find debugging a computer program needs surprisingly similar thought processes to studying a sonnet by Shakespeare.*

R3. *I can't claim paper qualifications. I've learnt all I know on the job.*

R4. *All of them, really. As you see, I got my PhD (Doctor of Philosophy degree) in software development from the University of Woodburn. My MA (Master of Arts degree) from Bristol was actually awarded for a thesis on the application of database technology to the optimisation of stock levels in retailing.*

These replies cover a complete spectrum.

R1 suggests the ideally qualified canidate. Provided all qualifications are held as claimed, there is not a lot more to question at this stage except, if wished, to probe further the bridge between qualification and job:

□ S. **Which parts of your degree course have you found of most value in your work, and how?**
□ S. **Has the DMS (Diploma in Management Studies) improved your management in practice, and if so, how?**

Before leaving the subject, we will want to throw in a remark such as:

□ S. **It's company practice to see all qualifications as a condition of final acceptance. I presume that wouldn't cause any difficulty for you?**

Studies have suggested that the proportion of qualifications falsely claimed by candidates is higher than might be thought.

R2 is clearly stretching facts as far as they can go, perhaps further. However, there is nothing really wrong in this in the circumstances; the candidate is doing his best to answer a question that doesn't fit his CV well. It invites a probe which must test mental agility and communication skills, and even, possibly, sense of humour:

- ☐ S. **That's interesting. I don't know Shakespeare's sonnets as well as I would like, but please explain the similarity with debugging a program.**

R3 is frank, but we may learn a lot about motivation, commitment, attitude to well-qualified colleagues, and family circumstances by a follow-up such as:

- ☐ S. **Have you ever considered getting a qualification by part-time study or distance learning, and if so, what conclusions did you reach?**

The answer to this may be the starting point for several probes or supplementary questions.

R4 is a fascinating answer. We have not heard of the University of Woodburn. We suspect it is a degree mill in the American midwest, but we may be wrong. The facts can easily be checked in any good reference library, but the attitude of the candidate must be explored now:

- ☐ S. **I'm sorry, but my knowledge of American universities is rather patchy. Could you tell me about Woodburn?**

This may bring a frank statement immediately.

R4. *Actually, it's a degree mill. You send $1000 and they send you a great, big, garish certificate.*

- ☐ S. **But you claimed it as a relevant qualification?**

R4b. *That's just my way of getting back at interviewers. A bit of a joke really. You passed with flying colours, of course.*

Our reaction at this point is likely to depend on our personality and our powers of forbearance.

If the candidate claims it as a genuine qualification, we would probably do best to note his replies for follow-up afterwards. Our suspicions might be unfounded, in which case our ignorance would be better hidden.

As for the claimed degree from Bristol, that will be covered by our check on qualifications.

☐ 10. **What do you** not **have that we need for this post?**

R1. *Well, I'm not sure that I could handle your micros without training. Of course, I don't know about your product range. And I would have to get to know the people I would be working with, and the customers.*

R2. *Detailed product knowledge and experience of the company procedures.*

R3. *Nothing.*

The answers to the question can almost be evaluated by weight. Any candidate who produces a long list demonstrates lack of confidence. Anyone who suggests he knows it all is brash and trying to deceive himself and you. R2 is close to the right balance.

Expectations in regard to pay and conditions

In selecting our list for interview, one of our criteria should have been the salary history of applicants. If we include someone who is already on a higher salary we run a serious risk of wasted effort. Unless their paperwork suggests exceptional suitability, or we are very short of candidates, the same will be true of anyone who is on a much lower salary.

Questions in this area are almost always asked, but may in reality be a cheat. If they have any function for the interviewer, it can only be to open the process of salary bargaining while he is in a position (because the candidate is still the supplicant) to exercise undue pressure.

Some recruiters choose to advertise no salary level, but to trawl the market. While objections may be raised against this approach, if it is adopted, questions are more legitimate.

☐ 11. **What salary do you require?**
☐ and 12. **You know what we're prepared to pay for the job. I take it you would be prepared to take it for that figure?**

R1. *I haven't thought about that, but I'm sure it wouldn't prove to be a problem.*

R2. *Something about the figure you advertised is fine.*

R3. *Currently I'm on 9½k. But if I took this job, travelling would cost more and I would have added responsibility. I have another offer of 11k which I like the look of, so I'm really after no less than 11½.*

R4. *This may be a problem. I have been offered 11½ already. I much prefer the job here, and was really looking forward to joining your team, but I can't altogether ignore the career progression aspect. I do hope there is some scope for discussion on this.*

R5. *Salary is not the most important thing as far as I'm concerned. Job satisfaction and compatibility with the team I work with mean much more. However, I owe it to my family to do what I can to keep up with the rat race, and I certainly would not come for less than I'm getting now. I feel sure that, if you want me, you will offer a fair figure.*

In view of the comments made above, it may be appropriate not to take the replies too seriously, although most will give some evidence.

R1 is a sad, passive, nearly desperate reply. From someone who is unemployed, we would be wrong to judge harshly. From someone apparently in a satisfactory job, it suggests serious problems which have hitherto not been discussed. In this case, we may probe:

☐ S. **You sound anxious to get away. Are there problems?**

R2 is defensive and cautious, probably indicating simply that the candidate is embarrassed. Prolonging the embarrassment is unlikely to achieve anything, unless other evidence (his current salary, or some throw-away remark) has given us particular doubts about salary. In such a situation, we must stick with it:

☐ S. **You are quite sure about that? We both need to be clear where we stand on this one.**

R3 is pushing too far at this stage. It may be a statement of fact, it may be a crude attempt to bargain, or it may be designed to impress us with the candidate's selling skills. We need to try to find out which:

☐ S. **Oh, I'm rather disturbed to hear that. We have our own salary scales here, and have to think of our existing employees. We would have the greatest difficulty going**

above the published figure. It may be best if you accept the offer you have.

If the candidate maintains his position, it is a move towards a crunch. If we are not too bothered, we may feel it best to say so now:

☐ S. **Well, in those circumstances, I guess there's not a lot of point in prolonging matters. Thank you very much for coming. Shall we call a halt there?**

The candidate may climb down, in which case we will probably continue with the interview but reassess his bargaining skill. Alternatively, he may add something like R4, in which case we will take the story from that point.

R4 sounds genuine, and is likely to be the response of a highly credible candidate. If our other evidence suggests that we are likely to want him for the post, we are on the spot:

☐ S. **Yes, that is difficult, but there may be some. But it's a shade too early to look at that. Do you mind telling me about the other offer, and when you have to reply?**

He may or may not enlarge much about the other offer, but if it is genuine he will say enough to show this. He should certainly indicate the urgency of the situation, to which we may reply:

☐ S. **I see. I've noted that. Let's put it into cold storage until we've finished our other points, shall we?**

R5 is the classic reply. It is either from a book or a good candidate, but judging which will need the help of other data.

7
THE PRESENT:
PERSONAL CIRCUMSTANCES

Overall objectives

1. To ensure that there are no personal factors which would make it difficult for the candidate to carry out the job required.
2. To seek additional indicators which might help to show the suitability of the candidate for the post.

The areas which may be explored include:

- Family situation and responsibilities
- Health and disabilities
- Outside interests and activities
- Self-image.

We may, rightly, hesitate to explore the non-working life of a candidate. Indeed, certain aspects – race, colour, creed, sex – are covered by law. But all aspects of life affect all others; it is impossible for anyone to separate their personal and working lives. Physical and mental health in particular have a clear, direct effect on work performance.

Sensible exploration of those parts of the non-working life which clearly impinge upon work is helpful to the candidate just as much as to the employer. But we must explore tactfully and sensitively, covering only those areas which may be relevant.

Discrimination

Our exploration of personal circumstances must not discriminate unfairly against particular candidates.

The law is involved in this area. It is dangerous, for example, to raise issues with a candidate of one sex which we do not raise with candidates of the opposite sex. If, for example, we ask a female candidate whether she is planning to have children, or what her husband thinks of her application, we must ask the complementary questions of male candidates, and interpret the answers in the same way. Better still, we should steer clear of such ground, to avoid any danger of misunderstanding.

Other kinds of discrimination may not be unlawful, but their use is difficult to defend logically, and they are only likely to make a correct choice harder.

The commonest of these is age discrimination. The frequent use of age brackets in person profiles is, in nine cases out of ten, based on crude stereotype thinking ('Everyone over 40 is too set in his ways' etc) which has no more validity than racial stereotypes ('West Indians are all stupid'). It is a pity that age is one of the few aspects of the human being it is possible to measure precisely. Were this not so, more of us would realise that (a) everyone ages at different rates – some are older at 30 than others at 60; and that (b) a wide spread of ages brings balance and breadth of experience to any team.

It is possible to discriminate against any unwanted candidate simply by selecting questions we believe he will be unable to answer. This technique may be used by biased interviewers in an attempt to justify their preconceptions. There is no way its use can help effective selection.

Family situation and responsibilities

Questions in this area are most likely to arise if the post would involve relocation. These are discussed in Chapter 8 (page 118).

It is particularly important to avoid any questions which can be seen as having a sexist connotation. Questions such as:

□ **Are you thinking of starting a family yet?**

should *not* be asked of any candidates unless, for some reason, they are asked of candidates of both sexes. Even this is risky.

Questions about children are sensitive, and while they may reasonably be asked of any candidate who appears to have the care of young children, the same approach must also be taken with candidates of both sexes.

☐ 1. **I notice your husband/wife has a job too; how does he/ she feel about you possibly getting this post?**

R1. *He/she has always accepted that my job comes first. I'm the breadwinner; he/she works for pocket money and family holidays. We sorted this out before we married.*

R2. *We would have to have a serious talk. It would require a lot of thought.*

R3. *There are several possible answers. We are a liberated couple, and take a relaxed view of each other's concerns.*

R4. *We have decided that I would take it, and he/she would resign. It's my turn; the last time, it was the other way round.*

Any credible reply that indicates the matter is under control must be acceptable. It is not for us to judge someone else's domestic life. However, if doubt and uncertainty are suggested, we are entitled to be concerned.

R1 and R4 seem to pass this test, but R2 and R3 raise doubts. R2 especially is unsatisfactory. The impression is created that the matter could be in serious doubt. We must probe:

☐ S. **You worry me rather. From the way you answer, you haven't discussed it with each other, but you feel there could be serious doubt. Am I right, and if so, when do you think you might resolve this?**

We would probably be wiser to restrain any curiosity answer R3 might arouse, but try to pin matters down more closely if we can:

☐ S. **So you are quite certain that, one way or another, if we offered you the job there would be no problem?**

☐ 2. **Has your wife/husband looked round the area yet, and if so, what does she/he think of it?**

R1. *Not yet. We'll do that very quickly if I'm lucky.*

R2. *She/he came with me today. I'm expecting her/his report when we've finished.*

R3. *We spent last Saturday here. She/he really likes it; we have cousins who live just down the road, so it's not entirely strange country.*

The interpretation will depend on whether the question is asked at first or final interview. At first interview, it would be wrong to take any reply as negative; this is merely an area in which bonus points may be scored. At second interview, however, replies are much more significant.

R1 gets no bonus at first interview, and a minor black mark at second.

R2 and R3 both score the bonus, and R3 helps us to feel more comfortable if we are thinking of offering the candidate the post.

☐ 3. **I see your son is 15. Where is he with his exams?**

R1. *He's away at school, so provided we can keep him there, what I do shouldn't affect him.*

R2. *He's taking this GCSE next year. I think everyone takes it now.*

R3. *He's working for GCSE. Yes, as you imply, this is a problem. My husband/wife thought about it a lot, and we have decided that, if I get the job, we shan't move home until next summer. It's not ideal, but then it might take that time to sell the house, anyway.*

This is a genuine problem, and the question has two aims. The direct aim is to establish if the boy's education might prevent the candidate accepting the post if it were offered, or worse still, accepting and then finding problems serious enough to affect his work or cause him to leave. The indirect aim is to probe the candidate's maturity and common sense.

R1 satisfies the first aim, but contributes nothing towards the second.

R2 is worrying, and satisfies neither. If we remain interested in the candidate, we may decide to stimulate his thinking:

☐ S. **They do. Do you feel it might disturb his preparation for the exam and his chances of success if you were to move home in the middle? How would you tackle this?**

R3 sounds the right one, although the situation will remain an anxiety for him and us.

Health and disabilities

The area of health is one that interviewers may be reluctant to enter, but it may be helpful to do so in the interests both of employer and potential employee. In doing so, we must remember we are laymen and never pretend otherwise.

☐ 4. **(The company requires a medical for all new recruits.) Health OK?**

R1. *Fine. Haven't seen the quack for years.*
R2. *I don't know of anything.*
R3. *OK now as far as I know, but I did have some trouble 18 months ago.*
R4. *I've had asthma since I was a child, but otherwise I'm fine.*
R5. *I had an operation on my neck six months ago, and I'm under radiotherapy at the moment. I go to the infirmary for an hour every four weeks.*
R6. *I spent three months in Welton five years ago, but doc says I'm fine these days.*

We must resist the temptation to act as an amateur physician. There are anxieties enough attached to health, without our adding to them. Our role is solely to assess whether there is prima facie evidence of a problem so serious that the selection procedure should be varied or stopped short.

R1 and R2 clearly offer no such evidence, and we must pass on.

R3 justifies a straightforward probe:

☐ S. **May I ask what the trouble was?**

The least show of reluctance to answer this suggests we should pass on tactfully; the candidate has been told about the need for a medical, and should he fail it, he will suffer.

Any answer will put us in the same situation as R4, or possibly R5.

R4 may prompt us to ask question 5 below, or we may throw it over to the candidate:

☐ S. **Do you feel this might be a problem in the job?**

This could be followed, if appropriate, by a minute or two analysing any relevant differences between the candidate's current situation and the post in question.

R5 appears to suggest a serious problem. We must again remind ourselves that it is not for us to judge, and that the candidate probably already suffers some anxiety. However, as employers we must choose a sensible approach. A typical way forward may be:

□ **S. Uh huh. If we decide we would like you for the job, maybe it would be a good idea if we got you to see the company doctor before you handed in your notice. What do you think?**

Whatever answer is made, we have offered help, and the ultimate decision will be ours anyway.

As Welton is a mental institution, R6 is hardest of all to handle. We must put any bias as firmly behind us as we can, pass on and, if we decide the candidate is in other respects the person we want, we must await the medical report before deciding.

□ **5. What time have you had off for sickness in the last couple of years?**

R1. *None.*

R2. *Three days last February, and a day, I think it was, the previous autumn.*

R3. *Not a great deal. Just flu and things and after I got a liver bug in Majorca.*

R4. *I was off for six weeks in the summer with back trouble, but not much else.*

R1 and R2 cause no problem, and reference to his current employer will check their accuracy in due course.

R3 could imply a bad record of time off for minor ailments – the kind of employee for whom the health record is a major job factor. We can try a probe, or may decide to wait for the reference, as such people may genuinely lose count of their days off sick. But the problem must not be forgotten.

R4 may take us back to the previous question 4, if it was not used. If it was, we may probe.

□ **6. Do you suffer any disability?**

R1. *No.*

R2. *Nothing that affects my work.*

R3. *I'm rather deaf, but I wear this aid.*

We will not usually ask this question unless we have reason to do so. Serious disabilities will usually be clear from the start, being mentioned in the contacts before interview. Minor disability may be a source of embarrassment, but may also affect work, and we are entitled to be aware of it.

R3 justifies the probe:

☐ S. **Have you found it a handicap at work at all?**

followed by a discussion of any relevant differences between the candidate's present situation and the post in question.

☐ 7. **I see you mention epilepsy on the form. Has this been much of a problem, workwise?**

R1. *The only real problem has been with other people who don't know much about the condition.*

Epilepsy, like several other conditions, may cause more trouble through the ignorance of others than it does directly to the sufferer. As responsible employers, we must ensure that we are aware of the facts, and so are any employees who might encounter a sufferer in their job.

Our reply to R1 will need to make clear that we are one of these.

☐ 15. *I can quite understand that. Our people all know the facts. We have a couple of other epileptics, and we've made sure they know the situation.*

☐ 8. **I couldn't help noticing your limp as you came in. Nothing serious, I hope?**

R1. *Twisted my ankle yesterday playing football with the lad.*
R2. *I've a touch of arthritis. Premature ageing, I expect.*
R3. *One leg an inch and a half shorter than the other, thanks to Gerry.*

R3 only might justify a probe.

Outside interests and activities

When interviewing students and others who have not held a full-time job, it is especially important to gain an insight into the motivational system of the candidate (to see how naturally active he is in mind and body) and to learn of skills and knowledge that might be relevant to the post to be filled. In such cases, these factors may provide some of the best predictors available, and this area of questioning should be pursued very thoroughly.

They can also be valuable when interviewing people who are currently unemployed. Denied the outlet of a full-time job, how do they use their time, energy and skills and seek self-fulfilment?

For all candidates, outside interests may add significantly to our understanding.

☐ 9. **Tell me about your pop group.**

R1. *Well, it's not mine really. I just go down and play the drums when the regular lad's not there. It's an excuse for a good night out, really.*

R2. *Couple of my pals started it three years ago. Pete is our lead player, and Karen does the vocals. I play the guitar. We get quite a few pitches now.*

R3. *We call ourselves the Tealeaves. Country and western stuff, but we've worked out a sound of our own. I'm business manager; I keep sober and drive the van. It's getting quite big; we're fully booked until June, and cutting our first disc next week.*

R1 and R2 do not help, hinder or suggest the need to probe further.

R3 sounds interesting, and could be positive or negative. The message is that the candidate has a strong entrepreneurial flair, which may not be used in his employment. Our reaction will depend on (a) whether the post in question might use such flair; and (b) whether it seems that the group might take time and energy that would be needed by the job, if we appointed him. Probing is needed:

☐ S. **How do you find time and energy for it all?**

☐ S. **The post does involve some travelling, as you know. Might this create a problem?**

☐ 10. **What reading have you done lately?**

R1. *Not a lot. It's hard to remember ... Mostly science fiction.*

R2. *I got hold of a copy of* Spycatcher *recently. I found it quite boring after the first couple of chapters.*

R3. *I've discovered a writer called E V Lucas. He wrote a lot of essays about the time of the First World War. It's only light reading, but it conveys the flavour of English middle-class life at the time really vividly; I feel I've been there almost. I've managed to put together a complete set now.*

We are not assessing just anyone's reading habits with this question; we are looking at the reading of people who thought it worth putting 'reading' down in their application. In doing this, they have implied that they see it as an activity which they are reasonably proud of and prepared to be questioned on. We are justified, therefore, in using their reply as evidence, if we can.

R1 suggests that 'reading' was a cop out; an activity that filled a blank space on the form and sounded respectable.

If this is correct, it also implies the absence of other constructive spare-time interests. This may not, of course, be a negative factor. Many people with young families, demanding jobs or invalid relatives have neither time nor energy for active leisure. But if none of these (or an equivalent) is the case, then we may doubt how positively the candidate views life in general.

R2 may or may not convey the same message as R1. *Spycatcher* (or some other trendy read) may have been mentioned as a positive choice, in the spirit: 'Have you seen it yet?' But it too might have been a cop out: 'The only title I can think of.' The probe is easy:

□ S. **I haven't read that one. What else have you been reading recently?**

R3 sounds the sort of thing we are looking for: enthusiasm, positive choice, active understanding. To be sure, we may use a similar probe:

□ 11. **How do you find your magisterial duties fit in with work?**

R1. *Not too much of a problem. We only have to do a certain minimum number of sessions a year.*

R2. *It takes about two days a month, on average, on regular days of the week. But we can also change days if we need to to meet work requirements. Emergencies of one sort or another crop up occasionally. Does your organisation have a policy on public service?*

The question of public service is one we must be clear on. Magistrates and councillors have quite heavy demands on their and their employers' working time. Employers may take the view that, in allowing this, they are contributing to the effective running of the community of which their organisation is part. They may feel there could be benefits in having a voice within the local establishment, or having someone around to sign passport applications. But, especially when choosing new employees, they may feel that such duties cannot be combined with effective performance in the job. This will, of course, depend partly on the nature of the job.

A realistic, consistent and clear view is essential, so that they, the employees concerned and others who may have to bear a share of the extra work all know where they stand. Grudging and partial acceptance will not work.

R1 is worrying, as it sounds rather less than frank. The probe might be:

□ S. **How many days did it actually take over the past 12 months?**

R2 throws the ball, correctly, into our court, and requires an answer. If our policy is not to encourage such activities, we will need to say so, adding:

□ S. **In view of what I've said, how do you feel about your application for this job?**

The interview may terminate there, or we may receive an assurance, which must be noted and referred to in any subsequent offer letter, that the public duty will be resigned.

□ 12. **Has your Action Group succeeded in its aims?**

R1. *It hasn't really been very active. It started at a meeting last October, but I haven't heard anything for a month or two.*
R2. *They wrote to the local councillors and our MP. They then got posters printed, and quite a lot were put out. But I'm not*

sure that anything has actually been changed. Democracy doesn't seem to mean much in our neck of the woods.

R3. *Not yet, but we've made some progress. We had the Minister down with some of his people and we made a presentation to them. It went well, he promised to examine the case, and we got a lot of publicity out of it. Picture of him and me on the front page of the local rag and so on. But there's a lot to do yet.*

Real involvement in local action demands much commitment, but is less likely to intrude on employment than holding a public office. The skills, determination and knowledge necessary to achieve any measure of success may sometimes overlap with the demands of the person profile. If this is true in the post we are filling, we may probe an activity such as this to gauge the depth of involvement and the likelihood of such commitment being transferable:

☐ S. **How did you get involved with the Group?**
☐ S. **What has been your personal contribution to the Group?**
☐ S. **Have you done this sort of thing before? If you have, please tell me about it.**

☐ 13. **How would the Drama Society get on if you accepted this job?**

R1. *I'm sure they would find another Chair.*
R2. *That would have to sort itself out. My job comes first, and the Drama Society will survive without me – better, no doubt, than with me.*
R3. *There's a vice Chair, who would be only too happy to take over. I should be sad not to see the move to our new theatre; we've put a lot of work into that. But I'm sure the project would not suffer; we always made a point of delegating and involving everyone. After all, I'll still be in the same country.*

The replies to this may have more direct relevance than the more personal questions. As the senior honorary officer of the Society, the candidate has a big responsibility for its success. His reaction to the possibility of letting it down may indicate a lot about his working morality and conscientiousness.

R1 is trivial, and leaves a negative impression. We may feel we should probe, for example:

□ S. **How about the move to the new theatre you mentioned earlier?**

R2 shrugs the problem off. It may have been faced more responsibly than appears.

R3 sounds excellent, and gives considerable confidence.

Self-image

Our self-image is a valuable indicator of our personality. It may differ widely from how others see us, but it will often be closer than any impression that can be formed at interview. The insight we display and the way we describe it can also be good indicators of maturity and balance.

We must beware of posing as amateur psychologists in exploring this area. Our purpose is legitimate; to assess the reliability and predictability of the candidate at work. But tools and time are limited, and any questions we ask with this aim can only supplement the overall impression we build up from the CV, the other replies and the references.

□ 14. **How might one of your closest and best friends describe your character?**

R1. *Ah. Well. Honest, friendly, helpful, good at his job ... How will that do?*

R2. *I've never really asked them. Intelligent, conscientious, reliable, plodding sometimes, but gets there in the end.*

R3. *Extrovert, energetic, ambitious, go-getting, definitely not over-modest.*

R4. *Highly articulate, creative, talks too much maybe, self-opinionated, very intelligent, arrogant occasionally, but usually manages to hide it.*

The replies to this question often show remarkable truth, as far as they go. As with real references from other people, what they do not say is often more important than what they do say.

The more they square up with the impression we have formed in other ways, the more likely they are to show the insight of genuine maturity. When we hear an answer that contradicts other evidence, we must weigh the possibilities either that the candidate is immature or that we have misjudged him.

R1 will probably do very nicely, thank you, and lists most of what we ourselves would say in that candidate's favour.

R3 admits its own bias. What it says is probably right enough, but will not match many person profiles. It is the answer of someone who has not yet entirely grown up.

R2 and R4 sound helpful and relevant, and will probably complement our other evidence, while giving additional demonstration of maturity.

◻ **15. How might your worst enemy describe your character?**

R1. *That's a tough one. I really don't know. Maybe he would say I was unambitious.*

R2. *May I plead the fourth amendment? No? I think he might say I was over-sensitive sometimes. Perhaps touchy on some subjects. But he would admit I was superb at my job.*

R3. *He would probably attack me for being a company man. He might try to suggest I worked too hard for my health. Not much else he could say.*

R4. *Inhibited, introvert, quiet, withdrawn. But he'd be wrong, of course.*

This question will always be less revealing than the previous one. Perhaps surprisingly, candidates are happier at putting frank statements about their failings into the mouths of hypothetical friends than enemies. Nevertheless, we may gain additional evidence from some replies.

R1 probably clinches a view we had already formed.

R2 may add data we had not yet got, and is also almost too defensive in tone, suggesting a hidden fear. There may be some skeleton, real or imagined.

R3 is so flippant it further reinforces the impression of immaturity, perhaps of some unreliability.

The hypothetical enemy of R4 is almost certainly not wrong, despite the attempted disclaimer.

◻ **16. Tell me something that makes you really angry.**

R1. *Not much at all. I'm really quite calm usually.*

R2. *I don't suffer fools as well as I should.*

R3. *I nearly said being asked a lot of personal questions, but luckily I stopped myself. Ha ha. Unnecessary delays, I think. Late trains. I'm a very impatient person, my wife tells me.*

R4. *People who end by saying 'OK?' Yes, and excessive noise.*

These answers add a little more evidence to our assessment. We may feel we can believe all of them; for some reason, anger is not always seen clearly as a sin or failing. As with other personality questions, however, they will not tell the whole truth; only what the candidate wishes to reveal.

R1 confirms the impression of a candidate who is mature and balanced; his enemy might say so balanced as to be motionless. But if sturdy absence of reaction is on our person profile, this candidate will be a strong contender.

R2 is probably truthful and may support other evidence.

R3 goes over the top. He and his interviewer have probably begun to suspect that they are not made for each other, and might even say so before too long.

R4 suggests some nervousness. As amateurs, we would be out of order to use the word neurosis, but we would be alert to other signs which might point the same way.

8
THE FUTURE

Overall objectives

1. To learn about the candidate's longer-term career plans (if any) and how they match with the present application.
2. To learn how career, private life and plans for leisure link together in the longer term.

The view the candidate holds of his longer-term future may help our selection in several ways. It may show the quantity of his thought and personal planning and give additional insights into his motivational system. It is therefore worth exploring, although answers must be hypothetical, and even more open to flights of the candidate's imagination than in other parts of the interview.

This is an area of particular importance with candidates such as students who are near the start of their career. With such people, it is reasonable to expect they have given much thought to the future. Also, in the absence of a track record, future plans will assume more importance in providing evidence on which to base our selection.

Long-term career plans

Not everyone has thought deeply about their long-term career objectives. It is, indeed, something that is rather too easy to talk about on the spur of the moment. However, we may learn more from those who have given the future serious thought, and may mark down those who have not.

□ 1. **We've already discussed your career to date. What are your career objectives and plans for the future?**

R1. *I want to get on. I have a family to support, and that is my objective.*

R2. *I'm at a crossroads. I feel I have exhausted the scope of my career in computing, at least in this part of the world. The time has come for a new direction, and if it succeeds, well I've plenty of time yet.*

R3. *I've given this a great deal of thought and done a lot of research on it. There's no doubt in my mind that the future lies in plastic technology, and that's where I want to be. There's a shortage of the right people, and those who've got what it takes won't stand still long. I'm going to be one of those.*

R4. *I've decided to go further up the specialist ladder. I enjoy using the skills I have, and I want to develop and make the most of them. I need more qualifications to achieve what I have in mind. I've just started an MBA by distance learning. When I have that, in two years, I shall be knocking on the door for a directorship. After that, who knows?*

R1 says nothing that can help us positively, and suggests that the candidate has not given, or is incapable of giving, much serious thought to the subject.

R2 tells a little more, although most of this would probably be evident from the CV or other replies. It includes nothing to suggest careful thinking and clear objectives.

R3 aims to create the impression of sensible analysis and deliberate planning. However, it actually succeeds in sounding superficial, and lacking in credible interest in the content of the job. It cries out for probing:

□ S. **How did you do your research?**
□ S. **What skills and qualifications will the 'right people' have?**

R4 sounds a very good answer. The plan is clear, credible, and soundly based in achievements already made. The claims are (subject to checking) supported by the action of enrolling for the MBA course. The only danger in such an answer might be the threat it could pose to the interviewer or one of his colleagues.

How they might react to such a threat is beyond the scope of this book.

□ **2. How would this post fit into your long-term career plans?**

R1. *It would be a good step up, and get me going again.*

R2. *It would broaden my experience, and give me the chance to prove myself in the direction I want to go.*

R3. *I believe it would be just right. It would use the skills I already have, but be sufficiently challenging to give the opportunity for development. With two or three years of this work under my belt, I believe I would have the right background for further growth.*

R4. *I've been hoping for the chance to work in your organisation for a long time. The reputation it has for training its staff is second to none. Once someone has done well with you, the world is their oyster.*

This is not an easy question for the candidate. For most candidates, the truthful answer is simply that it is a rather better job than they have at the moment, either because it pays more money, or because it gets them away from an uncomfortable situation. This is, of course, perfectly legitimate, provided that:

(a) it is not palpably drawing the candidate into a cul-de-sac from which escape will be difficult or impossible; and

(b) he is not purely or mainly planning to use our organisation as a means of career development.

R1 is flat and of no interest. It leaves the feeling that the 'step up' might be more than the candidate could manage.

R2 and R4 both cast the interviewer's organisation in the role of a charity for the development of flagging careers.

R2 creates the suspicion that the experience broadening may not really be part of a plan, but either opportunism or desperation. This impression will need to be compared with the evidence of the CV and other answers.

R4 goes too far in its attempt to butter the interviewer up; we are not that naive. It also carelessly makes clear that the candidate would be looking outside again as soon as he felt ready. We want at least the show of commitment, however uncertain it might prove in the event.

R3 is a clever and tactful answer, steering carefully between Scylla and Charybdis. It manages to sound convincing, and we can note it and check against other evidence.

☐ 3. **If you were to get this post, how long would you plan to stay with us?**

R1. *That's very difficult to say. I hope I should satisfy you, and that I would be with you for many years.*

R2. *I'm a loyal sort of person, and I don't like changing more than I need to. If the job is as challenging as I'm sure it is, and the opportunities for development within your organisation as great as I believe they are, it may well be a career-long commitment.*

R3. *Two years minimum in the job. After that, I shall be wanting to press on. But if I've sussed out your operation correctly, there'll be lots of headroom here for the right people.*

This question may sometimes be no more than the shadow boxing of interview convention, serving more to embarrass the candidate than to produce additional evidence, least of all about how long he is likely to stay. But the replies may throw up something that will confirm or counteract impressions we have built up.

R1 is passive, thinking only of how we may react to them. It displays no drive or ambition, but there is a desire to please which may match certain person profiles better; if all our staff were wildly ambitious, the organisation would soon be reduced to chaos.

R2 has fielded the question correctly, and in consequence we have learnt little or nothing.

R3 may ring warning bells, but is probably more brash than bad. We may feel inclined to probe, or at least tail twist:

☐ S. **So we'll need to get the best out of you within two years, before your motivation flags?**

☐ 4. **Where do you see yourself, jobwise, in ten years' time?**

R1. *I hope I will be a section leader by then. Maybe a manager like yourself.*

R2. *Ten years is a long time. I hope that will give me time to realise most of my career goals. I would like to think I should either be a director or a consultant by then.*

R3. *Ten years ought to give me time to grow within an organisation that provides the right nourishment, such as I believe your own to be. I think that with the further training, and good management, I have it in me to reach board level, I would hope within the manufacturing function.*

R4. *I would like to be head of my own, dynamically growing company. Selling my own widgets and knocking the spots off the competition.*

We have gained nothing from the question by receiving reply R1, except confirmation that that candidate sees a career as, with average luck, a gentle upward stroll.

R2 claims to have career goals, something we will cross-check with previous answers or probe now:

☐ S. **What exactly are your career goals?**

R3 adds the goal of growing within the manufacturing function, which could be important, the realisation he needs additional training and good management, and a touch of flattery. It adds up to a reasonably encouraging answer.

R4 is interesting, especially if we sell widgets. From a younger candidate, it sounds a particularly appealing answer, apparently showing drive and relevant ambitions. Should it prove accurate, both we and the candidate might experience a number of years of considerable mutual benefit before any crunch could come.

From a candidate in mid-career, it sounds rather different. If credible, we may feel it to be threatening, and if incredible, it will be line-shooting.

Whoever says it, it offers the opportunity for a useful discussion. We must probe:

☐ S. **That's fascinating, even a little frightening. Tell me how you would go about realising this ambition.**

The reply, guided by further probes if needed, should help not only to assess how realistic the statement might prove, but also to show more of the interests and strengths of the candidate.

☐ 5. **If you were to be appointed to this post, do you feel there would be any additional qualifications or courses of study that might be helpful to you, and if so, which?**

R1. *Not really. I would want to concentrate on picking up the job.*

R2. *In the course of time, yes. I think training in structured programming would be particularly helpful, and I would like to go on a course of advanced software design.*

R3. *Well, yes. I understand your organisation sometimes sends people on MBA courses at Harvard. This is one of the reasons I'm so keen to work for you.*

This is a question that candidates may have failed to anticipate, and is likely to get an unrehearsed reply that may be revealing.

R1 may be fair enough, but suggests a lack of upward thrust which may clash with claims in more rehearsed answers.

R2 sounds thoughtful and positive, and inspires confidence.

R3 goes too far at a first interview. Our organisation is unlikely to be a training charity.

The link between career and private plans

This takes the investigation of the future a stage further. It may produce deeper thinking or wilder fantasy; probing it will give us some evidence of the candidate's quality of thought, even if his answers are not objectively very significant.

☐ 6. **The interaction between career, family and outside interests is often a problem. How would you like to see these fitting together in your own long-term life plans?**

R1. *You're right. My husband/wife had to give up his/her job when we moved the last time, and he/she has only managed to find a part-time one here. That's one reason why we're so keen not to move a second time.*

R2. *My work comes first, of course. But I'm Chair of the Community Association this year, and I don't want to let them down if I can help it. That's why I'm looking for something that will not make too many demands on my spare time, or take me away from the area.*

R3. *We agreed a long time ago that my career comes first. As long as that is going well, other things will go well, and can be fitted around it. This seems to have worked, and it remains our strategy.*

R4. *For us, the key is the children. We want to give them the right start, which to us includes university if they're good enough. My spouse and I enjoy our careers immensely, and so far we've both been able to pursue them at the same time. But in four years' time, with Richard reaching the fifth form and Eileen only a year behind, we shall have to rejig things for a few years. However, it's much too early to say how that might work out. For now, the signals are green, and it's full steam ahead for both of us. As for leisure, we see that as an aid to the full life, not the life itself; we use a lot of it to keep fit and work off the stress.*

Candidates will usually claim that their career comes first, for obvious reasons. Among these replies, R1 is too vague to interpret clearly, and although R2 makes a statement about this, the remainder of what he says simply serves to cast doubt on it.

R1 indicates no clear thinking or planning. It suggests a hand-to-mouth approach.

R2, as has been said, implies that the stated order of priorities ('my work comes first') is not the real one. The Community Association appears first, at least for now. We may not welcome this, especially if the post in question calls for long hours or travel. On the other hand, it suggests strong commitment and a good level of achievement in a spare-time activity. Replies to other questions may indicate why this is so, what it tells about the candiate, and the chances of the post in question tapping these skills and interests.

R3 is simple and straightforward; other evidence will help to indicate its credibility.

R4 seems the reply of someone who actually has thought things through, and who has also fully involved, as such planning must do to be meaningful, his partner. Its wording suggests a high-level candidate at every point. It helps to give confidence that the application would not have been made unless it was a genuine part of a careful plan.

□ 7. **What would be your reaction to someone who suggested backing you to set up your own business?**

R1. *I would be flattered, but I doubt if I would pursue it. I have been too long as an employee. It wouldn't be practicable at my stage of life.*

R2. *I should be tempted to go for it, if he had the cash.*

R3. *Utter amazement, I think. I believe I am a professional, and have a great deal I can contribute to the right organisation, but I'm not an entrepreneur, and don't want to become one. For me the solid and, I hope, inspired professionalism; for someone else the risk-taking.*

R4. *Not today; I'm not ready. But in five or ten years, that could just be the ticket. I've a lot to learn from, and a lot to give to, other organisations for a long while yet, but one day that will be exactly what I'm after.*

Drive and entrepreneurship are not the same, but it is certainly impossible to have the second without the first. The replies must be judged in this light.

R1 probably doesn't help. It may quite well be a reasonable statement in the candidate's circumstances, which we will judge from other evidence. If, however, it is not supported by the CV (eg an age of 30 and a total career of ten years), we may feel justified in marking down.

R2 is too thin to say anything by itself. If supported by other answers, we may be inclined to accept it, or we may think it worthwhile to probe:

□ S. **How would you go about it?**

R3 is a good answer, which tells us that the candidate's drive is better assessed by other replies.

R4 is a very positive reply, especially from a younger candidate. It appears to show strong but well-controlled drive, something we will note and compare with other replies.

9
THE AWKWARD CANDIDATE

Candidates, even though they come to us seeking a job, are not all angels. They may display any number of a range of awkwardnesses. We may feel that those who do this do not deserve consideration. But some of these faults may have no relevance to the person profile, some may be purely temporary, and some may have been brought on by the tension of being interviewed by us.

We must have techniques ready to deploy against such awkwardnesses. Not every case will be suitable for treatment by questioning, but we will usually try that first.

The problems we may encounter include:

1. Shyness and talking too little
2. Talking too much
3. Excessive nerves
4. Trying to dominate
5. Using sex
6. Evading the issue
7. Lying and unacceptable deceit.

Shyness and talking too little

Perhaps the fault has been ours. We should mentally review all we have done, said or failed to do or say that might be the cause of the problem. We may have:

- failed to introduce someone present (possibly we have failed to explain who *we* are) or to explain his role adequately, with the result that he is felt as a threat.

- asked a difficult or embarrassing question before the conversational flow was established.
- said something without realising it that has puzzled or upset the candidate.
- talked so much ourselves that the candidate feels he is not really expected to say very much.
- overwhelmed the candidate with an excess of information, however relevant.
- cowed the candidate by expressing our own strongly held views on a particular subject.

Teenagers

The very worst problems tend to occur with some teenagers, who may be at a time in their personal development when relating to all adults is difficult, and who may have had no previous experience of an interview.

The form of the questions is even more important with shy young people than with other candidates. Most adults, when posed a closed or yes/no question, will enlarge on their answer without further prompting; shy young people will not, and we shall be faced with an unending string of monosyllabic answers.

Sample questions

The best starting point, as with some adults, is to get the candidate talking on *anything*, however irrelevant. We should go as soon as possible, therefore, for one of the candidate's declared interests – if he has declared any.

☐ 1. **What about United, then, eh?**
☐ 2. **What are the Newsboys going to do now they've lost Dusty Rhodes?**

If no interests have been shown on the paperwork, it is probably *not* effective to probe. A question such as:

☐ 3. **What do you do with your spare time?**

may be resented, or draw an answer such as:

R1.*Oh, just doss around. Discos, pub, that sort of thing.*

But we must only follow up a leisure interest if we have some knowledge and interest in the subject ourselves; young people dislike being patronised more than anything, and pick it up with lightning rapidity.

Whether this approach has helped or not, the move to the next area of questioning must be approached with great care. A wrong choice, or too sudden a transition, may spoil anything we have achieved. School or college is often a relatively easy subject for them, and has the added advantage that they are likely to see it as something in which we may have a legitimate interest. But exam results, even if good, are a conversation stopper. We might try:

- ☐ 4. **Why did you (not) stay on in the sixth form?**
- ☐ 5. **What projects did you do in the fifth form?**

As in any interview, encouragement will help, if we can find the right way to give it. Apart from positive body language and the best selection of encouraging noises, we can try such comments or questions as:

- ☐ 6. **That is most interesting. Will you enlarge on that for me, please?**
- ☐ 7. **Am I making my questions clear for you?**
- ☐ 8. **Good, excellent, please go on.**

The replies do not matter as such.

Talking too much

We tend to assume that candidates will be hard to get talking, but this is not always the case. Nerves or basic character may cause some to be almost unstoppable. With experience, we may be able to pick this up fairly early on.

Sample questions
- ☐ 9. **We are getting rather short of time. May we pass on, please?**
- ☐ 10. **Could you just summarise this phase, please?**
- ☐ 11. **Do you usually talk so much?**

The replies to the questions given above are unimportant. What we want is appropriate action.

Other ploys available include such old faithfuls as:

- shuffling papers, and reading them with attention

- looking out of window
- starting to take extensive, apparently verbatim notes
- looking at the watch/clock
- taking watch off and shaking or listening to it.

Failing success with any of these, we will be driven to say simply:

☐ 12. **I'm sorry, but time's run out. I have another candidate waiting. Can you find your way out?**

Excessive nerves

Excessive nerves may show in too much or too little talking. The many other ways they may show include:

- trembling, especially of the hands
- sweating
- tense, tight or unnatural posture
- frequent changes of posture and shifting of weight
- clenching of the hands or gripping furniture
- failure to make eye-contact
- talking too fast
- talking very quietly, or replies that tail off into inaudibility.
- failure to listen to the question.

All interviews produce some tension in the candidate (not to mention the interviewer). But there is a temptation to feel that anyone who shows excessive nerves must be a poor candidate. This may be correct, if the person profile for the post in question involves the ability to do well in interview-type situations, as with one-to-one selling, for example, or conducting interviews of various kinds. But if this is not the case, as is most unlikely with, for example, a VDU operator, a ledger clerk or a research chemist, we will need to persevere to establish the facts that *are* relevant.

Sample questions
☐ 13. **Which was the period in your career you enjoyed most? Please tell me a little about it.**
☐ 14. **Tell me something about your photography.**
☐ 15. **From what you say in your CV, you must have enjoyed your time at university. Please tell me about it.**

The way forward

In this situation, the replies to the questions do not matter as such.

Until tension has lessened, the questioning should concentrate on aspects we believe the candidate feels positively about, and which pose little or no threat. There are plenty of these to be covered in any interview.

The form of the questions should be as open as possible.

The impossible

At the end of the day, there are a few combinations of interviewer and candidate that just cannot work. As with some everyday relationships, the body chemistry is wrong. If it seems we are in this situation, we will need to realise it and do something about it; to soldier on will achieve nothing.

If this happens in a panel interview, we can quietly take a back seat. If the process includes (or can be adapted to include) further interviews at this stage, we should draw quickly to a close and brief the other interviewers on what has happened.

If neither of these alternatives is possible, we must think on our feet. If we would be the boss of the candidate, were he selected, then in the absence of special factors (rare skills, for example) we will not want to select him. If he appears (personal bias apart) a weak candidate, this problem will probably clinch the decision. But if his claims appear strong, we will have to devise some method of involving a colleague to whom he can relate more normally.

Trying to dominate

A few candidates will take as weakness our desire to listen, to give them every opportunity and to be as fair as possible. They may try to browbeat us, pressurise us, dominate us, or take control of the proceedings. We cannot allow this to happen. As interviewer, it is essential that we remain master, even though we do all we can to encourage and allow the candidate to put his case.

Sample questions

☐ 16. **Forgive me, but I would prefer to stick to my original plan. OK?**

☐ 17. **Thank you for your views. My wish is to concentrate on the area I first outlined. May we go back to that now please?**

☐ 18. **I want to be fair to all the candidates, and rightly or wrongly there is certain ground I wish to cover with each. May I take it that you do still wish to be considered for the post?**

Questions may prove ineffective in such a situation, and we may soon move to firm statements.

☐ 19. **I'm sorry, but I have very limited time. I must move you on quickly to the next point.**

☐ 20. **I'm sorry to interrupt you there, but if I am to consider you for this post, there are certain things I must know. The question I asked is one.**

☐ 21. **I'm afraid we are wasting each other's time, Mr Smith. Thank you very much for coming. Let me show you out.**

Fortunately, such situations do not arise very often.

Using sex

Interviewing a candidate of the opposite sex in a one-to-one situation poses potential problems, which may test our professional detachment. The aim of the candidate is to impress and please the interviewer. Also, in the course of any interview, it will be essential to explore the candidate's character and many aspects of his or her approach to life in depth. The situation is one of enforced intimacy.

Only a small number of candidates will set out to use sexual attraction deliberately. A lot of unsuitable people might seek the role of interviewer were this not so.

But a much larger number will use such attraction if they sense the interviewer is susceptible to it. Susceptibility may be difficult to hide, and is picked up instinctively by most people.

Almost everyone, however, when called upon to impress and please a member of the opposite sex, will use, subconsciously at least, a sexual component in their behaviour.

The antidotes
The situation is similar in many ways to that of doctor and patient, and similar approaches may be needed.

Professional skills. The best antidote must be experience and training that have developed a truly professional approach and the detachment that goes with it. This is in any case the aim in all aspects of interviewing of all candidates. Personnel officers and those who interview regularly must, to do their job properly, possess these skills.

Unfortunately, many people who must interview do so rarely, and have little opportunity to develop the professional approach. In this situation, we must not allow ourselves to be caught unawares.

Panel interviews. The problem may suggest the use of a panel, even if this was not otherwise necessary. If so, we may try to incorporate a member of each sex on the panel. This is a good idea for many other reasons as well.

The chaperon. We may decide it would be best to bring in a second person specially, if we sense a particular danger.

Self-knowledge. Whatever other steps we take, we must, if we are to make a correct selection, be aware of our own susceptibilities and biases.

Selecting the opposite sex
Some of us may be more inclined to appoint a member of the opposite sex. On the other hand, the majority probably react in the other direction, and shy away from such an appointment.

There are several reasons for this second reaction. We may feel that appointing a member of the opposite sex might expose us to the ridicule of our colleagues. We may feel it would expose us or our fellow workers to temptation. We may feel it would distract us in our work. We may feel our spouse would object.

Worst of all, we may have the belief that members of the opposite sex are less likely to be efficient workers, at least in our own, invariably 'special' environment. This is demonstrably wrong, and in fact unlawful. We must put such thoughts clearly and explicitly out of our mind.

Evading the issue

We must recognise deliberate evasion as soon as we meet it. It is wasting our time. Useful techniques in such a situation include:

Give time to focus. We must accept that most candidates need time to focus on a question, and usually feel the need to talk while they are doing so. It takes a strong candidate to remain silent while he thinks, and we must give all a reasonable chance, especially if we are trying to get the flow going smoothly. Patience on our part is essential and will save time in the end.

Is it deliberate? Some evasion is quite unconscious; the result of a woolly thought process, a bad choice of words, or a poorly worded question. We will need to decide if any of these are the case, and react accordingly. We may build it into our assessment of the candidate and pass on. If the subject is important, or the fault with our question, we will ask a differently worded question on the same subject.

Avoid interruption. Interruption in particular is unhelpful, and we should do it only rarely and when quite unavoidable. Questions like 25 should be very infrequent. If we find we have interrupted a candidate more than twice, something is going wrong, and we should ask ourselves (possibly the candidate) what it is.

Sample questions

☐ 22. **May we just go back on that one please? I'd like to hold on my original question for a moment.**

☐ 23. **Forgive me, but I must press this point. What I would like to know is exactly *why* you made that decision.**

☐ 24. **We seem to have wandered off the subject. May I bring you back to my question, which was what you saw as your greatest problem in that assignment?**

☐ 25. **Sorry to interrupt, but time presses. I must move you on to your next post, head of development. What were your responsibilities in this?**

Tough action. If evasion continues, either in one lengthy answer or over a long sequence of replies, we will feel we must act firmly.

☐ 26. **No, that doesn't answer my question. Please try again.**

☐ 27. **I sense you are evading the issue. Am I right, and if so, why are you doing so?**

Lying and unacceptable deceit

As in normal life, there is in interviews a thin and sometimes uncertain dividing line between acceptable and unacceptable deceit.

The black list

Candidates will bend every situation as far as it will go to what they believe to be their advantage. Interviewers expect them to do this, and the whole process of selection interviewing is framed to take account of it.

Some things will not do, however. These include misstating material particulars, such as:

- claiming false qualifications
- claiming incorrect salary levels
- incorrectly claimed periods of employment
- misstating age
- hiding dismissal or forced resignation
- hiding criminal convictions.

We must not worry unduly about the items on this list, not because they do not matter, and not because they will not happen, but because they are difficult to check at interview. We must develop a nose for such things, and when appropriate use techniques such as those listed below under 'The grey areas'.

The ultimate checks lie in other stages of the selection process, including:

- the use of a good application form, which includes all relevant questions and the warning that material misstatement may lead to dismissal if appointed.
- sight of all relevant documents, including birth certificate and qualifications, before appointment.
- careful taking-up of references, both written and verbal.

The grey areas

Some areas are on the borderline, and may be acceptable or not depending on how they are expressed, how far they are pushed, and how they match with other aspects. These include:

- overstating responsibilities
- incorrect statement of reporting lines
- overclaiming of achievements
- hiding serious problems.

These may at least partly, be picked up at interview, if we have studied the paperwork carefully and interviewed thoroughly, listening to, noting and comparing replies and probing when unsure.

Three kinds of clues may help.

Internal inconsistency. We must always be alert to the details of what was said, and how they match up. If we have any doubt, we must probe:

☐ 28. **You say you found management interference frustrating, yet I have a note that you told me earlier that you had bottom-line responsibility for the operation under the Board. How did this happen?**

☐ 29. **Sorry. I understood you to say earlier that you reported to the manufacturing director, but now you say your plan was blocked by the plant manager. Can you explain just what the chain of command was?**

☐ 30. **Why were you moved sideways, having just improved profitability by over 100 per cent, as you have told me?**

☐ 31. **I'm afraid I don't understand why you decided to leave without another job to go to, only six months after joining if, as you say, there were no problems in the job. Can you enlighten me?**

Inherent improbability. Common sense and our own experience must never desert us, even under the charm of a convincing candidate.

☐ 32. **It is very unusual for a new graduate to be given 'total responsibility' for such a large operation in his first appointment. Can you enlarge on exactly what that responsibility covered? Who was your direct boss, and what were his responsibilities?**

☐ 33. **You say you were one of 18 development engineers.**

Surely you didn't all report direct to the R&D (research and development) director?

☐ 34. If the conference was the success you tell me, why was it never repeated?

☐ 35. That seems an odd time to change jobs, just after a major success and a big increase in responsibilities. What had gone wrong?

Special knowledge. Occasionally, we may be in the happy position of knowing more than a deceitful candidate expects.

☐ 36. But surely National Servicemen were not given commissions in the RAEC (the Royal Army Educational Corps)?

☐ 37. Why did you leave Aberdeen University after only three years, when the degree course there lasts four?

☐ 38. I thought all pre-1980 BIM (British Institute of Management) Fellows automatically became Companions?

☐ 39. I'm sure my old friend John Smith would be most interested to learn of your responsibility for the success of his operation.

10
THE CONCLUSION

Overall objectives

1. To answer the candidate's questions
2. To give the candidate an opportunity to make final representations
3. To check that he still wishes to be considered
4. To make clear what the remaining stages of the process are
5. To offer the post to the chosen candidate, and to inform rejected candidates (if this procedure is adopted)
6. To leave a good final impression with all candidates
7. To pick up any final information.

This list may look long but all items, except the first, are usually brief.

1. Answering the candidate's questions

The candidate should have had several previous chances to ask questions. We will have given these during the introductory phase (Chapter 4, page 62) and the discussion of the present post (Chapter 6, page 90). However, it is essential that we also give this final chance. Additional questions may have formed in his mind as the interview progressed, or there may be points he has not found the opportunity to raise. The chance is even more important at first than at subsequent interviews, but we should always give it.

We must ensure that we have allowed sufficient time for this phase without undue haste. At first interview, between five and ten minutes is usually right, depending on the seniority of the post. At final interview, two or three minutes may be enough, as most points are likely to have been covered by this stage.

☐ 1. **Are there any points you are still not clear about, or any questions you would like to ask me, before we finish?**

R1. *No, nothing, thank you.*
R2. *Can you tell me about the perks? What would I get above the salary? Would I be paid for overtime? Does the job rate first-class travel? And the car; what models could I choose and would I get private mileage?*
R3. *We've covered nearly everything I wanted to ask, but there are just a couple of points. First, I'm not clear exactly what authority the post would have for hire and fire and industrial relations. Second, perhaps you can enlarge on the relationship between this post and the marketing director; is there a direct line, functional responsibility, or a purely advisory relationship?*
R4. *Can you give me a salary indicator, please?*

Conventionally, recruiters judge replies to this question by two standard criteria.

First, the candidate is expected to have some questions left to ask; if he does not, the feeling is that he may be less than seriously interested. This may not, however, be fair or right. It is perfectly possible that the interview has been so comprehensive as to cover all the points that an intelligent and seriously interested candidate might have.

Second, undue emphasis on salary and perks is often judged to be bad. The candidate should, according to this view, be principally concerned about job content and satisfaction, and think little about the quid pro quo. Clearly there is some truth in this, but it is a matter of balance, and will vary widely according to what information has already been made available.

If we have given no indication, for example, about salary, a question about this is not only reasonable, but indicates the candidate's serious intentions. On the other hand, questions about the fine details of perks do not sound good.

R1 fails the first test, but for the reasons given above, to mark it down in the absence of other evidence seems unfair. If, however, it comes at the end of a passive and unconvincing display, in which maybe the interviewer is aware that some important angles have *not* been covered, we would be fully entitled to take it as further evidence of weakness or lack of interest.

R2 concentrates on the fine detail of pay and rations. There are no job-related questions, and we may conclude that the perspective shows a lack of proper interest in things that matter.

R3 would conventionally be seen as a good answer. It appears to show that the candidate's main concerns are the true nature of the post and its responsibilities. However, convincing sounding questions are one of the easiest things to plan and rehearse when preparing for an interview. How much faith we pin on such a reply will depend on how it matches the evidence we already have.

R4 will be interpreted according to the amount of information we have already given in the advertisement and during the interview. If we have given little or none, it is highly relevant, and not to ask it would be an omission which indicated either lack of serious interest, an over-anxiety to please, or perhaps undue timidity. Indeed, if it is not asked, we will probably wish to pick the point up ourselves.

□ 2. **By the way, I don't think we've touched on salary. If we were to offer you this post, it would be somewhere in the range of 10 to 12k. How do you feel about that?**

R1. *Fine, no problem.*

R2. *As you know, I'm on 10½ at the moment. From what I have learnt of the job, I do see it as a clear increase in responsibility – one that I welcome very much – and I would like to hope that you would be prepared to appoint at the top end of that range.*

R3. *Well, I've been looking through the ads for other jobs of this type, and the going rate is somewhere between 13½ and 18. I saw one in the* Sunday Times *at 21k. Admittedly it was in London, but in other ways it was identical to yours. It was this kind of remuneration I was looking for when I applied, and knowing the reputation for fairness your organisation has, I felt sure you wouldn't let me down.*

R4. *Not happy. You didn't state a salary in your ad, but the fact you called me to interview seemed to suggest that you would be prepared to offer a good rise on my present pay. Unless you are able to go up to at least 14, I'm afraid I must withdraw.*

The way the question of pay is approached will depend to some extent on custom and practice in the organisation. Public bodies are generally far less ready to negotiate than the private sector. It will also depend on the amount of information on pay already supplied to the candidates and the stage selection has reached.

However, nothing can be gained by continuing the process if agreement on pay is unlikely to be reached, so we should be prepared to face the issue in some way whenever it may be raised.

How we interpret R1 will depend mainly on the candidate's present salary, if any. If we can offer a reasonable rise, or if the candidate is unemployed, the reply is quite straightforward. If, however, no rise would be practicable, we may wonder why the candidate is prepared to accept the situation without comment and seek an explanation:

□ S. **I'm afraid that means we would have to start you on a little less than you're getting now. What would you feel about that?**

R2 appears to be sensible and to call for whatever response the available headroom, our keenness on the candidate and the stage reached in the process indicate:

□ S. **Yes, I will note that point, and if we decide to offer you the post, we will certainly do what we can.**

R3 sounds like a crude and premature attempt to put on negotiating pressure, and may well be met by a fairly firm, possibly negative response:

□ S. **I'm afraid this is not the moment to negotiate terms. All I can say is that we will offer what we see as a fair salary to whoever we choose.**

R4 is clearly terminal, unless we feel the candidate is highly suitable. If we do, we may revise our ceiling there and then. If we do not, we may have to accept the closure:

□ S. **I'm sorry you feel that. Unfortunately, we are not able to go higher, as that would impact on our existing people. If**

that is your feeling, there is no alternative but to thank you for coming to see us and wish you well in the search for a suitable opening.

2. Final representations

There is nothing worse than the feeling, as soon as we have stepped outside the interview room, that we *should* have remembered to say so-and-so, or the regret that we were never given a chance to say such-and-such.

By the same token, the interviewer who helps his candidate to avoid such feelings will leave an impression of fairness and consideration in the latter's mind, and may also pick up occasional pieces of evidence that would otherwise have been missed.

□ 3. **Before we finish, are there any points that we haven't given you the chance to make, or anything else that you would like us to bear in mind?**

R1. *No thanks.*

R2. *Only to say thank you for a very fair interview and to hope I am offered the job.*

R3. *As I see it, you are looking for someone who can combine bookkeeping and computer knowledge with good management skill, plenty of drive and potential for the heights. While, as I said, my bookkeeping experience is a year or two old, I believe I fit your profile exactly. I believe the post you are filling would enable me to use my skills and experience to full advantage, and to make a real contribution to the success of your organisation. Thank you very much for your time, and I look forward to meeting you again, soon.*

R4. *Well, when I answered your question about the way we tackled O&M assignments, I think I may have given the impression that we were sometimes rather superficial. If I did, I would like to correct it; in fact, we are always very thorough, I'm afraid I didn't choose my words well in that answer.*

R1 cannot be faulted as it stands. It may, however, be confirmatory evidence of weakness.

R2 is also polite and reasonable, unless we have already

decided the candidate is inclined to creep, when it would be further evidence on the point.

R3 sounds a convincing and positive summary, always provided, of course, that it squares with our own view of the interview.

There is a danger, however, that this candidate may succeed in palming off on to us a more favourable view of the proceedings than we had actually formed. This is a legitimate enough aim on his part, and his attempt is clear evidence of good selling ability, something which may well figure in the person profile.

With R4, the candidate has accepted our invitation, and we must resist any temptation to mark him down for doing just that.

How we do assess the reply will depend on how closely it matches our own perception of what happened during the part of the interview he mentions. If we did form the impression he describes, we may mark him up both for the substance of the correction and for sensitivity. If we did not, or he has missed the point in some way, we may be justified in marking him down.

3. Is he still interested?

We must not assume that, having met and talked at length to a candidate, he will remain interested in the post. As was said at the beginning, selection must be a two-way process. We may save much time, possibly avoid the loss of alternative candidates, if we check the strength of his interest before the candidate leaves us.

☐ 4. **Can I take it that you do still wish us to consider you for this post?**

R1. *Oh, yes please.*

R2. *Yes, I think so.*

R3. *Certainly. Having had this chance to meet you and learn more about your operation and what the post will entail, I am even keener than before. I am certain that this is the opportunity I am seeking.*

R4. *I have a doubt. The line of responsibility through the site manager is not what I had expected. Unless I have misunderstood in some way, my feeling is that I shall have to take it all away and think about it quietly.*

R1 adds nothing, unless we expected a negative answer, in which case we will have to probe:

- ☐ S. **You surprise me. From what you have said, I felt we had come to the mutual conclusion that the post was not what you were really looking for. Can you enlighten me?**

R2 sounds weak when real conviction was called for. It cannot be passed over. But the probing may need to be gently done, or the doubts may be covered up again quickly, and we could waste time and effort making an offer which is refused. We might try:

- ☐ S. **You sound a little unhappy. Perhaps there is some aspect I can help you with now, while we are still together?**

R3 sounds good, but is easy to rehearse and say. We must compare it with the impressions we have already built up.

R4 must be followed up, especially if this is a final interview. It might be no more than a manoeuvre to draw us into a premature and favourable decision. How we follow it up will depend on how keen we are on the candidate, how accurately he has understood the position, and how much flexibility we have.

If we see the candidate as a serious contender, and he has understood correctly, we may ask:

- ☐ S. **What is there about this arrangement that concerns you?**

Depending on his reply, we may continue at first interview:

- ☐ S. **That is how it is at the moment. I'm sorry if it causes you doubts. However, if that is your only concern, may I suggest we leave it for now? We will have an excellent opportunity to discuss it further if we are able to include your name on our short-list.**

At second interview, we may go on:

- ☐ S. **That is the situation, certainly, but we would be pre-pared to discuss adjustments with whoever we wished to appoint. May I say we have noted your view carefully, and if we decide to make you an offer, we will come back to you on that point? May we leave it at that for now?**

4. The remaining stages

This question may be a repetition of one asked during the introductory phase (Chapter 4, page 62), or we may add additional information to whatever was said then. In either case, repetition is useful, as it is quite likely that the candidate has not picked up or remembered what we said.

□ 5. **We have more candidates to see this week, after which we will be inviting a short-list back to meet the manufacturing director, the site manager and myself, probably during the last week of the month. OK?**

R1. *Yes, fine.*
R2. *I hope you will be able to make your decision fairly soon, as I have another offer in the pipeline.*
R3. *Unfortunately I'm in Kos for two weeks starting on Saturday. I hope this won't prevent you considering me, as I'm very keen on the post.*

R1 is straightforward.

R2 may or may not be the truth. It may simply be an attempt to bring pressure to bear on us. The situation is similar to that discussed in Chapter 4, pages 66–7.

On the other hand, if we are at final interview of someone we judge to be a highly suitable candidate, we may need to be more forthcoming, while still refusing to be pressurised:

□ 15. **Thank you for telling us. There is no reason why our decision should be delayed, and if we decide to make you an offer, I will certainly contact you within the next two days at most.**

R3 is a nuisance, but if we may want the candidate, we must work round it. A week's delay is a small price to pay for the right person who may, in any case, be on several months' notice.

5. Making an offer

Some selection procedures, when large panel interviews are used in the public sector, or perhaps when the choice is made by one person within a smaller organisation, may include making an on-the-spot offer.

The advantages of doing this include:

- A good candidate, who may have other offers, can be secured before the chance is lost.
- If the candidate rejects the offer, it may be transferred to another while all are still available.
- The process can be speeded up.
- Any necessary bargaining can be done much faster possibly more effectively, face to face.

The disadvantages include:

- All candidates must be held until the decision is make.
- There may be undue pressure on the panel to make a hasty decision.

☐ 6. **Mr Jones, we have thought very carefully about all you have told us, and decided that, subject to references and medical, we would like to offer you the post, at a salary of £15,000.**

R1. *Thank you very much. May I say now that I am delighted to accept and look forward to joining you.*

R2. *That's good news. Would you object if I discussed it with my spouse and slept on it before I answered you?*

R3. *Thank you. I had hoped you could include a car. Do I take it that you are not able to offer me one?*

R4. *Ah. In fact, I've been thinking very carefully about our discussion while I was waiting, and I've decided the post is not what I am seeking. Thank you very much for the offer, but I prefer to step down.*

R1 calls for no comment.

R2 makes a very reasonable request. We may reply:

☐ S. **If you would like to think about it for 24 hours, please do, but we would like your response by tomorrow evening, please.**

R3 may be the start of bargaining which we cannot avoid. Our response will depend on how much we like the candidate, whether we believe there are others nearly as suitable, and how much headroom our organisation can give us.

R4 may prompt us to probe:

☐ S. **Oh, I'm sorry to hear that. Would you like to tell us why?**

If we are very keen to get the candidate, we shall start to bargain, after hearing the reply to the probe:

☐ S. **That is very sad. The salary is tied to a large extent by what we pay to our existing staff, but we would be prepared to raise the offer to £16,000, if this would help.**

Depending on the outcome, we may inform the rejected candidates immediately, if they are still available, or later by post when everything is final.

6. Leaving a good final impression

In concluding an interview, we will be alert to the fact that our candidates may turn up later as customers, perhaps on the other side of the table. They are certain to be part of our wider public, and to know customers and other staff. If we do not choose them now, we may need them for a subsequent vacancy; possibly even for this one, if the first choice turns us down.

All this indicates that our farewells, however the interview has gone, must be courteous and friendly. We must conduct the candidate out of the room smilingly, ensure he has his belongings, and that he knows his way.

It is essential that we make no remarks that suggest how we view the candidate; even a cheery 'See you again, I hope' will be misinterpreted. Inexperienced interviewers may feel pressure to make some evaluative comment, but this must be sternly resisted.

☐ 7. **Well, there we are, Mr Jones. Thank you very much for coming to see us. Did you have a coat?**

7. The bitter end

Very tense candidates may only relax when they believe the final whistle has blown. Then, once in a while, if a reassuring, friendly presence is around, they may feel the sense of rapport we have striven for unsuccessfully throughout the interview, and open up with amazing frankness. This is an additional reason for a member of the panel to conduct the candidate out personally.

☐ 8. **Not too painful, I hope?**

R1. *No, very fair. I enjoyed it.*

R2. *OK, but I wasn't sure I got on the right wavelength with the chap in the corner. I thought everyone else was super.*

R3. *It feels better now. To tell the truth, I was scared they were going to ask what happened at Grey's. Anyhow, it's all over now.*

R4. *I get so nervous at these things. My shrink tells me that's perfectly normal, which is reassuring.*

Any attempt to follow up will need to be made with double kid gloves, and may easily fail. However, walking slowly down the corridor, or in the lift, we may feel it is worth trying.

R2 might suggest a follow-up.

☐ S. **Oh, yes, Bill is quite a character. He can seem rather formidable at first meeting. Heart of gold, really. Did he stop you putting your case as you would have liked?**

For R3, we might venture the gentle response:

☐ S. **Oh yes, I did wonder how things had been for you at Grey's, but I didn't like to ask. I guess they must have been pretty tough?**

For R4, something like this might have a chance of working:

☐ S. **Your shrink's a wise man. I hate being interviewed myself; I think we all do. What other good advice does he give?**

If, in any of these cases, we find we are able to keep the conversation going, we may be inclined to do so as long as useful information seems forthcoming. Time spent in the coffee bar over the road, or giving him a lift to the station, may be more useful than the interview itself.

Bibliography

British Institute of Management (1980) *How to Be Interviewed.* D Mackenzie Davey and P McDonnell, London.

British Institute of Management (1975) *How to Interview.* D Mackenzie Davey and P McDonnell, London.

Brown, Michele and Brandreth, Gyles (1986) *How to Interview and Be Interviewed.* Sheldon Press, London.

Fletcher, Clive (1986) *How to Face the Interview and Other Selection Procedures,* 2nd edition. Unwin, London.

Fletcher, John (1988) *Effective Interviewing.* Kogan Page, London.

Grummit, Janis (1980) *A Guide to Interviewing Skills.* Industrial Society, London.

Higham, Martin (1981) *Coping with Interviews.* New Opportunity Press (now Newpoint), London.

Hodgson, Philip (1987) *Practical Guide to Successful Interviewing.* McGraw-Hill, London.

Hunt, Gary and Eadie, William F (1987) *Interviewing: A Communication Approach.* Holt Rinehart and Winston, New York.

Modus Publications Ltd (1984) *How to Be Interviewed.* Harpenden, Herts.

Turner, J B W (1987) *Your Curriculum Vitae and Interview: Practical Guidelines.* Management Update Ltd, London.

Yate, Martin John (1988) *Great Answers to Tough Interview Questions: How to Get the Job You Want,* 2nd edition. Kogan Page, London.

Index